Extreme Heat

Library and Archives Canada Cataloguing in Publication

Allen, Jimmy, 1940-
    Extreme heat : a firefighter's life / Jimmy Allen.

ISBN 978-0-9781070-7-9

    1. Allen, Jimmy, 1940- 2. Fire fighters--Canada--Biography.
I. Title.

TH9118.A45A3 2007   363.37092   C2007-905317-3

The author and publisher are are grateful to Ottawa firefighters
Michael Booth and Jeff Wainwright for providing permission to
feature their work on the front cover. They also designed the
website www.jimmyallen.ca and have their own website:
www.webflashover.com. We'd also like to thank Kenny Redman
for front cover use of his 321 Impact font (kennyredman.com).

The author and publisher are also grateful to Ottawa Sun
Publisher Rick Gibbons and photographer Denis Cyr for
permission to reproduce the award-winning colour photograph of
an accident scene on the back cover. We are also grateful to Sir
Sean Connery for use of his image on the back cover.

We acknowledge the financial support of the Government of Canada through
the Book Publishing Industry Development Program (BPIDP) for our publishing activities.

ISBN 978-0-9781070-7-9
Published November 15, 2007
Manor House Publishing Inc.
452 Cottingham Crescent, Ancaster, Ontario, Canada, L9G 3V6
905-648-2193 wwww.manor-house.biz

Extreme Heat

Jimmy Allen

Home Fire Hazard Checklist

Working smoke alarm outside all sleeping areas.

Working smoke alarm on every floor.

Home fire escape plan.

Carbon monoxide detector (if there are carbon fuel burning appliances).

House number is visible from the street.

Cooking is not left unattended.

Smokers use safe ashtrays and don't smoke in bed.

Combustibles are kept away from furnace, heaters or stove.

Extension cords are not used in place of permanent wiring.

Electrical outlets are not overloaded.

Candles are never left unattended and stable, non-combustible candleholders are used.

Matches and lighters are kept out of the reach of children.

Usually, boys 3-10 years of age are the main culprits. Children's fire play can be many things:

Playing with matches or lighters.

Playing with the toaster, stove or furnace.

Burning items such as toys, paper or garbage.

Setting a fire to destroy something or hurt someone.

(Courtesy of the Ottawa Fire Services Fire Prevention Division).

Dedication

*This book is dedicated to Sharon,
my wife, my lady, my love and my life.*

She took the blows while I did it my way.

* * * * * * * * * * *

*Each fire, each death, each suicide,
takes a piece of your soul.*

Practice Fire Safety

Install smoke detectors.

Prevent false alarms by regular maintenance, change batteries or re-locate if necessary.

Develop an escape plan.

Test your smoke alarm at least once a month. Push the test button and/or use smoke.

Clean your alarm at least once a month with a vacuum cleaner.

Replace batteries each year. Use battery type listed on the alarm

Never store unnecessary flammable liquids in your house and never, ever, store propane cylinders in your home.

If Fire Breaks Out

Remain calm.

Sound a warning. Dial 9-1-1. Summon the fire department

Get everyone out.

Never open an interior door without first checking to see if it warm.

If you should awaken to a smoke-filled room, stay low, crawl below the smoke to safety.

Close doors behind you as you leave the building. This will slow the progress of fire. If its safe to do so, turn off all appliances.

If you hear the smoke detector or hear someone shouting FIRE immediately evacuate the home.

Meet the firefighters when they arrive.

Decide on a meeting place outside your home.

Make certain that everyone in your home knows NOT TO RE-ENTER a burning building.

If you live in an apartment building develop an escape plan.

If someone requires assistance, assign a family member to assist him or her.

Make sure your babysitter understands your fire escape plan.

(Courtesy of the Ottawa Fire Services Fire Prevention Division)

Prologue

Somebody up there must like me. Otherwise, I would never have been spared to reach fire department retirement age and senior citizen status. I just hope it isn't the guy with the pitchfork, leaving me here to fatten me up for the red-hot coals.

I spent 39 years as a firefighter, and loved every minute of it. God, how I miss it!

Today, I can't go into a fire station for a visit and leave in under three hours. Firefighters are something special.

Donnie Gagnon was the most special of all to me. Donnie died at age 46 and I'm sure the toxic fumes he inhaled hastened his death.

Donnie's brother, Johnny, is now a District Chief and he's one of the ranking experts in the world in HazMat – hazardous materials and chemicals. He's consulted by security agencies across North America and around the world.

I'm not a writer and I told this to all the people who urged me to write a book about my dangerous, and sometimes hilarious, experiences.

They said to me: "You may not think you're a writer, but you're a compelling storyteller. Just put your stories down on paper in a firefighter's language."

Best-selling author Peter C. Newman, military book author and journalist Tom Douglas, and Ottawa Sun columnist Pat MacAdam, urged me to scrunch down over foolscap with my ballpoint pen and get at it.

They called my stories "visceral" and "riveting". Tom Douglas said it was like reading Mickey Spillane.

I can't write like Mickey Spillane, J.D. Salinger or John Steinbeck, but neither could they possibly invent the pathos and comedy of a firefighter's life. They didn't walk the walk or climb the ladders.

I'm told that no other firefighter in Canada, or the United States for that matter, has written his (or her) autobiography. There have been movies made but the screenplays are pure fiction and not based on real life experiences.

When I started writing this book, my wordsmith friend, Pat MacAdam, said: "Jimmy, writing a book is easy. Getting published is like watching a glacier move." I sure have found this out. It's like trying to get a job if you don't have any experience. No one wants to talk to you. Big companies would send my work back unopened. In August of 2004, a company in western Canada said they wanted my work. It made me so very, very happy. I told them: "If you have this much faith in me, I'll go into action", and I did.

So, here goes!

You may find that the book jumps around a lot, but then, so does life on the fire line. Fighting fires is not an organized profession. You never know what's going to hit you next. My book bounces back and forth from the sacred to the profane, from heartbreak to gallows humour, from tears to laughter. It doesn't bounce back and forth because of poor editing or placement of incidents. It bounces because that's the way it is in firefighters' lives.

I made a promise to myself, to Donnie Gagnon and all firefighters, that if the book was successful I would buy a kidney dialysis machine in memory of Donnie and donate it to a local hospital in his name.

In closing, please forgive the profanity and the raunchy stories. But that's the way life is and was in a fire station.

Captain Jimmy Allen (Retired)
Ottawa Fire Department

Author's Note

You shouldn't be reading this book. I shouldn't have been able to write it. I should be dead. I know that for a fact. More than one doctor told me the toxin levels in my blood were ordinarily found in a corpse. I could have moonlighted as a poster boy for an embalmer.

But somebody up there likes me, and I lived to share these recollections with you.

The Early Years

Any day I drove to work, one of the Four Horsemen of the Apocalypse galloped alongside my car.

He was Death!

Most days I left him behind in a cloud of exhaust.

Some days I couldn't outrun the bugger on the Pale Horse. Those are days that haunt a firefighter all his life. Looking back, I marvel that I never thought the dark horseman had me in his crosshairs. If you thought that, if you regularly felt his hot breath on your neck, it was time to start thinking about another line of work.

* * * * * * * * * * * *

On January 4, 1960, I was hired as a firefighter by the City of Ottawa. It was an adventure to work with the calibre of men around me, many of them World War 11 and Korean War veterans.

I loved everything about the job. It gave me a huge rush.

We had an aptitude test, a physical and an interview, and if you passed all three you were hired. It helped if you played minor pro hockey or football, or if your Dad was thick with the Mayor or an Alderman. Today, they hire by the numbers – so many points for being a member of a minority, so many for the colour of your skin, so many if you are female. The only criteria missing are Handicapped and White.

The training period I underwent was seven tough weeks. Then I went to a station and my real training began. It was sheer magic for me and I never stopped learning. I was smart enough to know how dumb I was and how much there was to absorb.

No matter what gender you are – male or female – you need guts, strength and brains. You need to know enough arithmetic to figure out that a gallon of water weighs ten pounds and that a five-gallon pail of water weighs 50 pounds plus the weight of the bucket. You might have to carry that much up a flight of stairs.

All the college degrees in the world aren't worth diddley-squat in a fire station. There are no such things as male or female jobs, but if tests continue to get easier and standards continue to get lower, eventually you're going to get someone on staff who'll hurt you.

No Box Scores For Injuries

Firefighters don't keep box scores of their injuries. Mine rank up there at the top. There were others hurt more badly than me and they didn't make it. I did. I seemed to have a black belt in survival. The man with the scythe almost had me in his win column a few times. I didn't see any bright white lights or long white tunnels but I heard voices.

Did The Horseman Catch Up With Me?

I heard one strange, disembodied voice say: "Hit the pedal! We're losing this guy!" I kept looking around wondering whom they were talking about. It was me! I was on my way to the hospital in an ambulance. When we got there, I had an IV needle in my left arm, another one in my right arm, and I was wearing an oxygen mask. A nurse kept asking if I wanted a clergyman. My blood pressure was 280 over 126.

It was time to start planning my funeral. Would I die from a heart seizure? A stroke? Would I just go to sleep and never wake up?

After one trauma, my hair turned white overnight. The pigment in my hair had died.

Another time I was all wired and tubed up in a hospital when I saw a stranger dressed in green hospital scrubs standing at the foot of my bed. I knew he wasn't an angel because angels wear white and have wings. We looked at one another. He spoke first.

He said he was the doctor who had done my blood work. He said he wanted to meet me because the last time he saw results like mine was at an autopsy.

Was I dead? Was I dreaming all this? Was someone else really in the room with me, or was I hallucinating?

Finally, I realized he was for real. I was alive. The doctor told me that noxious gases I had inhaled had burned all "the fur" – all the hairs – from my nose and the passages leading to my lungs. He gave it to me straight. He said my condition was going to create problems for me later in life. He was so right.

An "Instrument Of Barbarity"

In his thriller, THE SIGMA PROTOCOL, my favourite fiction writer, Robert Ludlum, told the story of a poet who was asked what he would save if his house were on fire. The poet said he would save the fire, because without fire, nothing would be possible. Ludlum wrote that fire is what made civilization possible, but that it can "equally be an instrument of barbarity".

I wish I had said that!

This is where I come in! I was a smoke eater – a firefighter for 39 years. When I started out, all you needed was a strong back. I'll be darned if I'll say a strong back and a weak mind but a high IQ wasn't a condition of employment.

Different Strokes

Most people who know me realize I could have taken the wrong road into a life of crime. When you're brought up in a family with 11 kids and a house with a strange pervert who rented a room... but, that's a story for another time.

I learned early to find second and third jobs that kept me out of the Prescott Tavern and the Grads' Hotel. In spite of that, I'd often be drinking in the Belle Claire Hotel with bank robber Paddy Mitchell. The Belle Claire had a cast of hoods from old "B" gangster movies. They were harmless rounders, who kited cheques, engaged in fraud, scams, forgeries and small-time robberies. They were the forerunners to Jimmy Breslin's "Gang That Couldn't Shoot Straight." Two of them successfully knocked off a three-ton van, only to find it was full of vibrators – dildos.

If I hadn't taken part-time jobs I would surely have become one of them. I played drums professionally. I did high tower work, wiring buildings for Cable TV.

The hoods talked openly, even though I was sitting there, and knowing that I was straight. Paddy Mitchell was the Godfather and he went on to bigger crime – the "Stopwatch Gang" that terrorized U.S. banks and boosted about $15 million. Paddy is doing 65 years in a federal prison in Pennsylvania, and there, but for the grace of God, go I.

What was said in bars went in one ear and out the other. Eventually, most of those guys ended up as unwilling guests of Her Majesty in a federal or provincial lock-up.

When they were released, I'd get lots of visits at the fire station I was working in. A couple of my firefighter colleagues had pasts similar to mine. Others locked themselves in their offices when the hoods, some of whom were scary, showed up.

In the 1960s I was given a huge contract to wire a few high-rise buildings in Kingston, Ontario, near the federal penitentiary. I'd visit some of my friends who were incarcerated. One of them was a brother of one of my fellow firefighters, and was in for armed robbery.

He kept his nose clean in Kingston and was transferred to a minimum-security institution. He and another prisoner escaped. The pair got into the old crime rut but this time it was drugs – a new mind altering substance called cocaine, which my buddy once told me was harmless – just refined coffee beans. Yeah, sure!

They got a brainstorm – let's do a big score and then go to Mexico. "We'll live like kings there."

Their plan worked. They kidnapped a bank manager and got $100,000 in unmarked bills. Now, this was 1967 when 100K was like $2 million today. They got into the nose candy, became careless, and were caught. The two of them went back to maximum security in Kingston.

I went to visit my friend and he said: "Jimmy, did we ever screw up. That cocaine shit did us in. You know I've been a thief since childhood. I may be a thief and a bank robber, but I'm not the type to hurt anybody. This stupid kidnapping seemed like a good idea. When we had pulled it off, it was like a dream come true. Then the other shoe dropped. We got 100 Grand in cash, and like fools, we got into that cocaine shit. We were on the run, so we hid the stash under the floorboards of an old house in Kingston. Neither of us remembers where. We could have gotten a reduced sentence if this stupid, cocaine fried brain of mine would kick in, but it won't."

A few years later he became ill and died under mysterious circumstances. So if you ever buy an old house in Kingston, check under the floorboards. The money has never been found.

* * * * * * * * * * *

In 1962, someone had the great idea to inspect houses in the afternoon. We had two-way radios, which enabled us to remain in contact with the fire station in the event of a fire. So, from 1.30 p.m.- 4.00 p.m. we inspected homes and found potential hazards, like wrong size fuses and other electrical problems, poor storage of petroleum and chemical products and flammable material too close to a furnace.

In 1964-65, Ottawa developer Robert Campeau began building high-rise units, and this presented a whole new challenge. The Queensway, an east-west multi-lane arterial road, was well underway and it brought other problems and challenges. The experts designed it with little intelligent forethought.

The speed limit was 60 mph. There was no centre-dividing barrier separating three lanes in each direction, so in slippery, dangerous road conditions, cars and trucks crossed into oncoming traffic at 60 mph. We were constantly going to accidents. Inevitably there were injuries, and sometimes deaths.

Our Early Equipment Was Primitive

For the first hundred years of fire fighting, our battle dress changed little – a metal or a leather helmet with fur flaps for cold weather, rubber boots with some protection against glass and nails, and a canvas fire coat that could burn when it got hot enough.

Around our waists we wore a leather belt that held a hose strap and a hydrant key. Our pants were neither fire resistant nor fireproof. Flames and fumes could easily get under the fire coat and your whole body was basically unprotected.

The equipment we had was primitive – axes, sledge hammers and crowbars. We asked for a Jaws of Life rescue tool but were turned down by the City. The Canadian Legion came through with $27,000 and bought the first one for us. Now we had an invaluable weapon in our limited arsenal.

Our next acquisition was a rescue vehicle, which responded to every working fire.

Public relations and awareness were musts, and were given high priority – not only during fire prevention week, but year round in schools and community organizations. We were involved with Muscular Dystrophy as far back as 1948.

The police force has always had responsibility for recovering the bodies of drowning victims. We took it a step further and formed a water rescue unit. With all the rivers and canals around Ottawa, it made good sense. Our Kevlar water rescue boat, crafted from the same material used in bulletproof vests, was tough, strong and very fast. It could be launched in minutes.

Next, we became involved with hazardous materials (HazMat). Because of a new phenomenon – the threat of terrorism – a crew of my colleagues took special courses to make the city a safer place. They're my heroes. They are always first on the scene for major fires, explosions, chemical spills and suspicious packages and powders.

Every city gets only so many bangs for its buck from their fire service. We take any criticism that may come our way because we feel it's part of the price of being a firefighter. I have to admit I chuckle when I hear some people say firefighters are the only group besides hookers who get paid so much for spending so much time in bed. I don't know what it's like in other cities, only in mine. As firefighters, we do not bring any revenue to the city, as does the police department.

In the 1960s, Ottawa built two new fire stations with flat tar roofs and no air conditioners. We passed the hat and bought window air conditioners for both stations. Two years ago, one of my brothers became so fed up with the piece of junk he had for a pumper he invited the media to visit and see duct tape holding a fire truck together.

The City is making noises about closing some fire stations. This would be a retrograde move. Why? Firefighters do more than just fight fires. Lyle McLennan was an enlightened and far-seeing man. He was the last Chief to come up from the ranks. He was in Korea when he was 16 years of age but his mother had him brought home.

Chief MacLennan had the wisdom to position our various stations to minimize response time. Thanks to him, no station was more than four minutes away from a potential fire scene. He was a leader. All the Chiefs after Lyle until today, have been hired from other municipalities – good men – but we had better within our own ranks, like Dave Smith, Claude Poulin and Garry Wallace. For reasons I cannot fathom, the City went outside to find their Chiefs. I find it insulting.

My friend, wordsmith and mentor, Pat MacAdam, said to me in conversation, "Jimmy, you really think the world of your men, don't you?" I answered, "Yes, as far as I'm concerned, they can walk on water." Pat probably took my statement with a grain of salt. About six weeks later Pat's wife Janet collapsed, and Pat phoned 911. When you dial 911 you get police – they are usually busy – ambulance – over extended, and fire. Because of years of experience, fire call response times have been cut in half – at least.

Number 10 station firefighters were at Pat's condominium in less than four minutes to help Janet. Their job is bleeding, breathing, shock, stabilization and comfort. My brother firefighters did their jobs, and when the paramedics arrived, they transported Janet to the hospital. Later that night Pat phoned me and said: "Jimmy, I have some information for you. Your men *can* walk on water." It made me very proud.

* * * * * * * * * * * *

We responded to an accident on a bridge, involving an overturned car. When we disembarked at the scene, we were freezing, because our clothing hadn't had time to thaw out from the previous call.

A 1961 Chevy was on its side. I noticed a Fire Department sticker on the window and realized it belonged to a District Chief from another shift. The second car, the one that hit him, was full of drunken young punks who'd been boozing and partying. They'd been speeding and they were on the wrong side of the road.

The Chief's misfortune was that he ran out of milk for his morning coffee. He was in uniform and looking for a corner store.

We approached his overturned car. What a sight! The Chief had been decapitated and his head was missing. When the car rolled, his head went out the window and a guardrail severed it. We went looking for it and found it 50 feet away in a gully.

Good man, great friend, terrific family man – all gone because some drunken bastards decided to drink and drive. If you look up the word "mistake" in a dictionary, my photo is probably alongside it. Far be it for me to preach, because I've driven under the influence many times myself, before I smartened up. If you're going to drink, lock your keys in the trunk or give them to a friend. In the long run, it's cheaper to take a taxi and the roads will be a lot safer.

What a winter! I'm feel as though I'm getting old fast. I'm only 21 and I look 35. My skin is tanning like leather.

My hands are cracked and sore.

Home is bed, sleep and nightmares. We've had 17 fatalities so far my first winter on the job.

This Firefighter's Life

In the spring of 1962, the New York City Fire Department came to Canada to recruit firefighters. It was very flattering for a 22-year-old like myself to be approached by such a great department.

Out of curiosity, some of us went to see what was on the table and to find out if it was worthwhile. They had come up to Canada to hire big, strong firefighters who were already trained and used to fighting fires without air masks, and in all kinds of weather.

The wages they offered were better than what we were getting, and so were the benefits. It was something for a young man to think about. One of the things we asked about was the retirement age and the answer surprised me.

We were told we'd be hired from November, 1962, to November, 1982 – twenty years, and then be pensioned off. I asked: "Why 20 years?" The answer was that no human being should fight fires for more than 20 years, as firefighting is physically, as well as psychologically, punishing.

When you're young, you look at things in a different light. It wasn't until I reached my 50s that I realized the full impact of what the man had said. After 30 years and a multitude of injuries, dealing with fires, explosions, burn victims and cave-ins, your head becomes so messed up. We all deal with death differently. For quite a while, I drank too much. Then I got lucky and found the fellowship of Alcoholics Anonymous.

As you can see from this book, I stayed put, and my 39 years with the Ottawa Fire Department were the happiest years of my life. I was truly blessed.

* * * * * * * * * * *

It was May, 1962. I loved my job. I got paid for doing something I'd have done for nothing. The men I worked with were my heroes. I was just 22 years old and so grateful I had a job as a fire-fighter.

Our hoses were all in the tower drying. The pumper, aerial and Chief's car were gleaming. I was so wound up there was no sense trying to get a couple of hours sack time. You don't really sleep in a fire station. You lie down and try to rest, try to unwind.

I went out the front door of the station. The moon was losing its glow and the sun was beginning to rise over the horizon. Out walked our Chief, Tony McCarthy. He was 55 and looked 65. He walked with a slight limp from an injury he got at a fire six years earlier. His leg was badly broken and he very nearly lost it to infection. He was transferred to lighter duties, and could have gone out on pension but he missed fighting fires. He came back.

He said: "You're new here."

"Yes, Sir, I am."

"Where are you stationed?"

"#7, Sir."

"You had a bad winter there, didn't you?"

"Yes, Sir, seventeen dead. It gets to you."

"I know", said the Chief. "Remember, don't take it personally. You didn't start those fires. Your job it to put them out. Do the very best you can. Bust your ass. Follow your officers' orders and learn. Always stay scared and respect fire. If you're not cautious and scared, you'll die. It's just that simple."

"Chief, can I ask you a question?"

He said: "Sure! I don't know whether I'll answer, but go ahead and ask."

"Chief, we just had a fire and no one was hurt. There was a lot of damage, but otherwise everything went well. I hardly knew you were on the scene. Then we had that warehouse fire. We lost two workmen inside the building. I was scared shitless. You walked around, directing operations, not yelling. I was terrified. How do you do it?"

He said: "Good! Stay terrified. That way you'll live a long life. To answer your question, during the Second World War I was a tail gunner in a bomber over Europe. I lost lots of friends and got shot up. After I recovered from my wounds, they wouldn't let me be a tail gunner anymore, so I was trained to be a firefighter. After night bombings we might have six whole blocks burning. There was no water, because the water mains had been blown up. We had as many as 30-40 bodies piled up like cordwood. After all that, a fire in a warehouse or a house is small potatoes. Don't get me wrong. I take my job as Chief very seriously. Yelling and screaming only upsets men and they stay out of your way. They're of no use if they're hiding on the fringe. Respect is what men need and want.

They function as a team and work harder and better when they're treated with respect."

What did I ever do right in life to have the honour, privilege and pleasure to be near, and work with, a man like him?

Death Never Sleeps

Firefighters are on the job 24/7.

We have strange work schedules.

Every few weeks we pull a 24-hour shift and we're at the fire station for an entire day. If all our equipment is ship shape and things are quiet the Captain may tell us to grab some rest.

We also have days off.

Some neighbours found it strange to see me working around the house on consecutive days in the middle of the week. Often, I'd be asked if I ever went to work.

Death never took days off.

He worked overtime.

If he wasn't breathing down our necks at a fire, he was waiting in the wings tempting us with the easy way out – an end to all our troubles, stress and sleepless nights.

Death By His Own Hand

Suicide is the silent, unknown predator – a sidekick of the Fourth Horseman. It's fairly common in the fire service. I imagine it's the same in fire departments around the world. I could name 50 of my brother firefighters who have taken their own lives. But I won't.

I have too much respect for them. I know, first hand, what drove them over the edge.

I don't judge them, just as I don't expect others to judge me. I do not judge my late brothers because I've walked many miles in their shoes.

We all live lives of quiet desperation, and some are more desperate than others.

As the coroner used to say, their reasons were between themselves and God. I don't know of any other group with a suicide rate as high as ours.

Recently, I attended a reunion and I chatted with a young, 12-year veteran firefighter. He looked directly into my soul and asked: "Can we talk outside?"

We sat on a bench near the meeting hall. He told me that three years earlier he was hurting so much from a car accident that killed a mother and her three children that he went home with the intention of killing himself.

He went down to the basement, loaded his .22 rifle and "put the barrel on the edge of my left eye and waited with my thumb on the trigger to get tired and press it to end the pain. I had flipped out and I know you think less of me and that I'm weak."

I didn't think less of him and I didn't think he was weak.

Why?

Because I'd been there once myself. If he was weak, then so was I.

The Innocent Always Suffer

In 1962, I was 22 years old and had been a firefighter for less than two years.

We responded to a fire call at 3.00 a.m. We lost a mother and five little children because the drunken scumbag of a husband upset a petrol fired space heater.

When I thought of those poor little innocent kids, my heart began to crack.

I had to exorcise the demons that were overtaking my emotions and my reasoning.

My heart, head and feet directed me to a bar where I started pouring booze into myself.

Alcohol was the great panacea. It would make me feel better. It would make me feel like a new man, and then, I'd treat the new man with a few more belts.

I didn't know alcohol was a depressant until I went for treatment for alcoholism years later. I always thought it was an upper that would drive black moods away.

I lurched from bar to bar looking for Nirvana, for blessed release. I only felt myself becoming more and more depressed.

Finally, I couldn't take it any more. My head was ready to explode. I had so much anger, rage and depression bottled up that I wasn't worried just for myself. I was concerned I might just hurt someone who said the wrong thing to me or looked at me the wrong way.

Misery loves company and I was my own best company. So I went home and located my Cooey shotgun in the basement. I loaded it with # 4 shot, which would stop a charging moose in its tracks.

I cocked the shotgun and put the barrel in my mouth.

I hurt so much! The pain was so intense I began to cry, and with the flood of tears, I eased off the trigger pressure.

I removed the shell from the shotgun. To this day, I can close my eyes and still taste blue gunmetal.

I dropped to my knees on the dirt floor of the basement, and cried and cried until there were no tears left inside me.

Firefighters who don't cry, who can't cry, DIE!

Merry Christmas

Ah, shift work, wonderful shift work. In 1964 we worked a 56-hour week – days for 10 hours and nights for 14 hours. Sundays we worked 24 hours – from 8 a.m. Sunday till 8 a.m. Monday.

It is almost Christmas. We've had three deaths in the last two days. We'll be working our 24-hour shift tomorrow. It's Saturday night; time to howl, get a lot of beer in us, celebrate Christmas and life because life is to be lived and it's short – too short.

In the firefighting business it can be all over for you any day or any night. If you make a wrong move you can find yourself tits up.

We all meet at a favourite watering hole. There's lots of pub grub but food is not what we're after; we want the escape that alcohol provides. Some people think that all firefighters are big, rough and tough, but we shed red blood and cry real tears. Some people think we can handle anything that comes our way. Wrong!

If we're lucky, some of us can show emotion. Others lock it up inside and end up as alcoholics with bad marriages, and a few find the ultimate release – suicide.

During my first four years as a firefighter, six of my brothers took their own lives for different reasons – two died of carbon monoxide poisoning in cars in their garages, one hanged himself, one shot himself and the two others died by "causes unknown".

The beer is sliding down real good, and everyone is having a swell time. It's a beautiful, chilly evening outside, with a full moon. I've had a lot to drink – too much. I have a routine when I've had my fill; I take my car keys, open the trunk of my Chevy convertible, and toss the keys in.

Even drunk, this idiot realizes it costs more to break into his trunk than to take a cab home. Back to the beer, war stories and fun. I roll home at 3:00 a.m. and my alarm clock goes off at 6:00 a.m. Man, am I ever hung over, but it's a beer hangover and will soon pass. I have to get my ass in gear. My car, where's my car? It's at some hotel somewhere and it's a long three-mile walk to work. The walk will help me shake off my hangover, but it's going to be one mother of a long Sunday.

The snow crunches under my feet, but I'm in no mood to appreciate the sound. It's really quiet. Smoke and soot from chimneys is settling on the pure white snow. There isn't a footprint or tire track anywhere.

I arrive at the fire station at 7:30 a.m. and I'm beginning to feel human again. Our parade line-up is at 7:55 a.m. What a rag tag army we are. We must look like a recruiting station for Alcoholics Anonymous. But, hey, there's a price tag on everything. You drink, you dance, and you pay the piper.

Our Captain is a World War II veteran and his piss tank days are behind him. He belongs to A.A. He tells us: "It's close to Christmas. Have your coffee, clean up the station, and make sure all the equipment is clean and ready. Then go upstairs and grab a couple of hours shut-eye. I'll take the watch."

This means he'll sit at the watch desk. If a call comes in, he'll awaken us through the speakers. What a prince!

All the stations in the city are wired together. When one station is called out all the other stations know. We had the old corner box system so when an alarm was pulled anywhere in the city, every firefighter on duty knew. Loud and clear!

We are tucked in about an hour, when all of a sudden, the dorm door is flung open and in walks the Chief. He looks like a cartoon character with his buggy blood-shot eyes, ruddy complexion and huge gut that is straining to pop his shirt buttons.

He yells at me to follow him.

"Yes, Sir", I say.

We go down the stairs and I'm wondering what kind of shit I'm in. Did I do something stupid last night? What's going on?

The Chief says to his driver: "Let's go."

I think: "Where?"

I say to the Chief: "Am I going on fire watch or something?"

"No!"

"Should I bring my fire clothes?"

"No!"

I get in the back of the car and he asks: "Where do you live?" I tell him and he orders his driver to take me home.

"You just got married, didn't you?"

"Yes", I reply.

"Then go and get laid and I'll pick you up in two hours. Merry Christmas."

What a job!

Firefighters Are Somebody, Too

Some people think a firefighter is a nobody. He's only a firefighter. Maybe so, but he may just be the guy who's going to save your life. If you think a firefighter is a nobody, you haven't had to call the fire department to your house.

The fire department isn't the squeakiest wheel so it doesn't get the most grease. For my money, it doesn't get enough grease. Over my four decades, I saw the budget for police increase four times more than the fire department's. Buy them another fire truck! That's all they need. They don't seem to realize that the oldest fire truck in service is held together with tender loving care and duct tape. Fire trucks take one helluva beating, especially in sub-zero temperatures.

I wouldn't wish a home fire on my worst enemy, but I often wonder what the attitude of the elected politicians would be if one of their homes caught on fire around budget time. I think they'd be singing from a different song sheet. After 9/11 in New York, we could probably have asked for the moon. Sadly, it takes a crisis of titanic proportions to stir the people who control the purse strings. Me? I believe in preventive maintenance. It's no good locking the barn door after the horse is gone.

I used to joke I was one of those wild and crazy guys who ran into burning buildings and met rats running out. Once we came up against a bunch of mailboxes with sticks of dynamite all wired up and set to go off. It was during the Front de Liberation Quebec crisis in the winter of 1970 when misguided nationalists killed a Quebec cabinet minister and kidnapped a British trade consul.

Lucky for us, it was so cold the batteries and timers froze. There were a couple of sticks of dynamite in each mailbox. If they had gone off they would have turned the sheet metal boxes into grenades. Mailmen found 10 other boxes wired up.

One of the most dangerous places to fight a fire is in a hardware store. Paint cans explode like shrapnel. Ammunition – bullets and shotgun shells – spray every nook and cranny. Some chemicals and solvents react with one another. Put two tablespoons of Javex in a Styrofoam cup with brake fluid. Watch out! A Hardware store can burn for days. The fires that can be most harmful to your health are chemical fires. Feather pillows and mattresses are no problem. They're all protein and the fumes won't harm you. Drapes, sofa and chair coverings and rugs made from synthetics are toxic. Their fumes can kill you.

Things Go Better With Coke

It was a beautiful June morning. We got a call to a Coca Cola plant in Centretown at 5 a.m. We could see the smoke from a distance. Captain Frank Kenny and I went through the front plate glass door that I'd taken out with a fire axe. Our first job was rescue. Buildings are replaceable but people are not. I heard the sound of back-up fire trucks coming.

"What the hell is burning?" asked the Captain. It was toxic and had an oil base of some kind. This was fire fighting before air masks, so ventilation was key to finding the seed of the fire. The captain went one way and me the other, entering a big office filled with lots of smoke. I put an axe through a couple of windows to clear out the room, and hit the fire with the one and a half inch hose line we used.

The other firefighters were doing their jobs and we were getting the fire knocked down. Then I realized where the fire originated. A group of safe crackers had taken tarps from coke trucks and built a tent over the company safe they were trying to crack. When they blew the safe with nitro glycerine the tarpaulins caught fire and caused quite a bit of smoke, so they panicked and got the hell out of there. I went over to the safe and opened it with my hose key. There was $11,000 in cold, hard cash in that safe. Now this was 1962 and in today's dollars it would be worth $150,000. If I had been a bad cat, I could have taken the cash, put it in my fire coat, left the room with the open safe and started working in another area. Even a police detective told me later I could have taken the money and no one would have known.

WRONG! I would have known! I wasn't hired by the Ottawa Fire Department to steal. I was hired to fight fires and save lives. God knows I have many faults, but I don't steal. We were just doing our jobs, and when all went well, the satisfaction was gratification enough.

D.N.R.

2.30 a.m.

We got a medical call. D.N.R. What the hell does D.N.R. mean? I found out it meant Do Not Resuscitate. We had an elderly female in a nursing home who was having difficulty breathing. Over her bed was a sign which read 'Do Not Resuscitate'. We were new to life saving and frankly, not that well trained. It was the 1960s and we weren't in the same league as an ambulance emergency crew. We always did our very best, but we were rank amateurs dealing with medical calls in the infancy of our Rescue Service. Let's face it. Getting to the scene fast was important. Minutes, even seconds, counted. If we could get to a victim within four or five minutes, the patient had a better chance of living. If better trained medical personnel got there before us, we deferred to them. If we got there first, we started treatment, and in this case, we did just that. Rightly or wrongly, we resuscitated the lady.

Just Drive The Hearse

The dispatcher sent us out on a pump to a downtown intersection, in response to an accident. He also sent a Rescue unit in case it was an extrication case. We arrived first. It was the first time in my six years of fire calls and car accidents that I saw a hearse on the scene.

Then I realized the hearse was involved in the accident, and the driver was half in the bag. He was returning the hearse to the funeral parlour and stopped for a few quick ones.

We were happy no one was injured.

The hearse driver was the kind of person who shouldn't drink at all. He was rude and belligerent when the police officer asked him questions.

He was asked: "Do you own the hearse?"

He told the cop: "No, I just drive the hearse and cremate bodies."

The police officer said: "Oh, just how long does it take to cremate a body, Sir?"

The hearse driver answered: "About two weeks for a fat bastard like you."

It was the wrong thing to say. The cop placed him under arrest. He was given a one year suspension and a fine of $2,000 and costs. Good!

You're Dead

During a particularly bad fire, before face masks were standard issue, two of the men lost consciousness due to smoke inhalation. Four of us, including the two who were still out, were subjected to a battery of medical tests.

Blood work was done, and, according to the results, everyone was dead! The doctor said there was no way anybody could have that much carbon monoxide in his system, and survive.

Once again, against the odds, the Horseman was cheated!

Call The Coroner

We had a Code 9 – a working fire in Centretown in a rooming house, and people were believed to be trapped.

We pulled up to the rooming house and the fire was really rolling. Garry Wallace and I went through the front door, which was open. We didn't have to bust it in. Shucks!

Somebody told us the fire was on the second floor in room #4. This was old-fashioned firefighting in the 60s. We busted our asses trying to get up the stairs. We crawled low to suck in air close to the floor. We got to room #4 and Garry said he was going to throw a chair or something through the window. Then we started our circle check. I crawled along the floor, and fuck, was it hot! My lungs were taking a real shit kicking.

I heard the crash when Garry took the window out, and the next sound was him puking out the window. There was nothing funny about our situation but I wanted to laugh. Maybe Garry was puking all over the people huddled on the street. Maybe he'd hit the Chief!

The room cleared. Garry's chair-through-the-window trick ventilated the room quickly. Now at least, we could see what we were doing.

Garry interrupted his barfing long enough to yell: "Call the coroner." We'd found a badly burned man. We pulled down the ceiling and opened the walls to check for fire extension. The smell of burned flesh was overpowering. That smell straightens out even the most seasoned firefighter. We know when we lose somebody. We know.

Is it any wonder that a firefighter has a shorter life expectancy than an average citizen?

We have long shifts and broken sleep patterns. We eat lumberjack meals at the fire station. We deal with death from fires, car accidents and suicides. We gain weight and drink too much off duty.

I'm not complaining – just stating the facts. Sometimes I think my routine can be compared to parking your car for a week and then starting it up again, pulling away at top speed. Your stubborn body goes from sitting to sleeping to eating to drilling to training to running through burning buildings at top speed. It's a wonder we don't have a big letter "S" on our shirtfronts. But, hey, Superman I'm not. I bleed and hurt just like everyone else.

Fire Station Life

We responded to a call at a six-unit building, where the smell of gas was overpowering. There were two propane tanks turned on full blast in the basement. The kitchen gas stove was also turned on full. The thermostat was turned down and the door leading outside was left open. Thank goodness we got there before the furnace kicked in. One spark and WHAMMO, the whole place would have blown.

It was obviously a hovel for some very heavy drug users. They had the whole place booby trapped, with syringes duct taped everywhere so you'd walk into them in the smoke, following an explosion. The dresser drawers also had syringes sticking out of them. If you were unlucky enough to stick yourself you had to be tested for AIDS and Hepatitis. We were lucky, none of us had to be tested.

* * * * * * * * * * *

We brought two guys out of a burning building and one of them said he had to go back in because he had three packages of cigarettes and a bag of white stuff in his freezer. He also said he had a cat. Cats are low to the ground and, sure enough, his cat made it out safely.

There are some embassies I wouldn't enter today unless the Ambassador carried me in on piggyback. If you hit one of those armed high-tech doors with an axe you could get blown across the street.

A lot of firefighters didn't like going out on medical calls. They were squeamish. Stroke or heart attack victims don't defecate or urinate on purpose. They don't have control of their bodily functions.

We pulled up to a small single family home and found a 65-year old man on his back clutching his chest. He was choking on his own vomit. I cleaned his mouth, removed his upper and lower plates, and asked the Captain to radio for an ambulance. It turned out the poor old guy dropped after shovelling his driveway. His wife and daughter were doing aerobics with a Jane Fonda video. Too bad they didn't work off their excess energy shovelling the snow out of their driveway.

I learned early on that firefighting and lifesaving are not destinations, they are journeys. I learned early on that there was so much I didn't know, but there were experts out there we could count on. The gas and hydro companies were invaluable resource people and I often invited them to the station to conduct seminars and share their knowledge.

Like Henry Ford, I was smart enough to admit I didn't know everything but I knew people who did. The lessons we learned from the utility companies helped us save lives down the road.

The gas company told us about the properties of home heating and cooking gas. We knew then if we had to respond to a call at a tank farm or distribution point we'd be dealing with product that was delivered at 400 pounds per square inch. We learned that the flow was stepped down to less than one quarter of a pound per square inch when it went through a home customer's meter.

As far as we were concerned, in the early days CPR was just the name of a railroad. We knew nothing about heart massage and mouth-to-mouth. The hydro people probably weren't first to realize that if life is to be preserved you have to keep the victim breathing and his heart pumping, but they were first to show us how to do it.

Their demonstration saved a life almost immediately. We were on a fire call and the ladder on the aerial came in contact with a

14,000-volt power line. One of my mates, Jimmy Walsh, touched the side of the truck and was blown 20 feet into a snow bank. There were smoke circles five feet in diameter at the base of the aerial ladder pads.

Jimmy was clinically dead.

I refused to accept that Death had won. I was the first man on our department to attempt heart massage and mouth-to-mouth. Jimmy's teeth were clenched shut and there was no way I could give him the kiss of life. None of my early training equipped me for a situation like this. I flew by the seat of my pants and breathed through his nostrils. My brother firefighters and I put Jimmy on a stretcher in the emergency car. I kept on gently forcing air into his lungs through his nose during the short ride to the hospital. On our arrival, a nurse looked at Jimmy and said: "Leave him alone. He's dead." I said: "He's not dead. His chest is rising and falling."

A doctor came by and said the same thing as the nurse, and that's when I lost it. I can't remember everything I said but I said some pretty nasty things to the doctor and the nurse. I guess the doctor thought he had a wild man on his hands. I have a 49-inch chest, a 36-inch waist and I look like John Gotti. He must have thought the best thing to do was humour this crazy man, so he called for the cardiac paddles and gave Jimmy a couple of jolts. I thought that the last thing Jimmy needed was more voltage, but the procedure worked. A dead man rejoined the living.

I may have been the very first person to improvise on mouth-to-mouth and give a person mouth-to-nose. It made sense to me at the time. I didn't think it mattered what orifice you used as long as air was forced into the lungs.

What thanks did I get? The Deputy Chief wanted to can me for my abusive and disrespectful treatment of the medical staff. I was so pissed off with the Deputy Chief when I got back to the station that I punched the fender of an old fire truck. I put a helluva dent in it. After things calmed down, the Chief and I had a long talk. It was only then that he realized all we were trying to do was keep Jimmy

Walsh alive. I'm a very hotheaded person and, like most others, I really care about people. All my brother firefighters do.

Jimmy lived. He was in a coma for six months. I visited him often in hospital, talked to him, shaved him and prayed for him. He snapped out of the coma, returned to active duty and stayed on until his retirement. Today, in his early 60s, he runs marathons.

There Are No Male or Female Jobs

One day, over a few beers in a tavern, the conversation drifted to what the qualifications were to be a firefighter. Everyone had his say and when it was my turn, I told them I had a father who was years ahead of his time.

We were eleven kids, and we were taught from the very beginning there was no such thing as male and female jobs. We all cooked, sewed, cut grass, shovelled snow and contributed financially. I said that the only things required to fight fires were guts, strength and common sense.

At 3:00 a.m., in a smoke filled room, it doesn't matter who's with you – male or female. We all dress the same and you wouldn't know one from the other.

If you have two out of three qualities, it's not going to work. You must have all three or you should look for another line of work. Firefighting is just too important a profession to take lightly.

Weirdoes

Weirdoes set fire to garbage bins and dumpsters and then get their jollies watching us extinguish them. People who pull false alarms just don't realize what they're doing. They couldn't care less if someone gets hurt. Sometimes we'd see the same guy lurking about at different calls. He wasn't your ordinary fire buff. He was a Mickey Mouse arsonist. Maybe it gave him a rush. Somebody ought to take a peek in his ear.

The dumbest pukes on earth have to be some arsonists. I can tell you 20 ways to set a fire that is virtually undetectable but I won't. I'm not writing a handbook for someone who wants to do a torch job. Most of the arsonists use an accelerant that can easily be traced. The dumber ones spill some on themselves and set themselves ablaze and they can be smelled 10 blocks away.

Over almost four decades, I saw an emergency service evolve and grow from a service that only swung axes and pointed hoses to a multi-faceted emergency department. We began to inspect homes and businesses to head off potential fires. We inspected one rental unit where the occupant was trying to barbecue a goat in the kitchen, using a tank of propane. He had the front and back doors open. I rolled everything out and threw it into the backyard. He was enraged. He didn't want to barbecue outside "because it might rain".

He was living in public housing, and I sailed into him about smoke, soot and grease damage to the ceiling and walls. He laughed at me: "The city will find me another unit to live in."

In some houses, we found cans of paste wax with rags jammed in before the cover was re-applied. That's a sure fire recipe for spontaneous combustion.

We found other houses that had fuse boxes with twice the number of recommended amps. We found carelessly stored alcohol, gas and kerosene.

Some of the houses had 30-year old newspapers jammed in the walls as insulation. They were squeezed up against old, frayed wires. Then they wonder where their house went. Some immigrants played the race card with us. That might have worked on someone else but not on me. I wouldn't roast a pig if I visited a Muslim country. Other immigrants were afraid of uniformed men and didn't want to let us in.

Some people gave us a hard time. They'd tell us: "I'm not leaving my propane tank outside. Somebody will steal it." They just couldn't get it through their heads that even the smallest leak had the potential of turning a propane tank into a bomb. Propane gas is heavier than air, drifts down to a natural gas furnace pilot light and POW, it's all over for the people in that house. Some people took the attitude: "I don't care about damage, the City will find me another housing unit."

* * * * * * * * * * *

We thought home and office inspections were just something for us to do between calls. Wrong! Numbers don't lie. These inspections actually cut the number of fire calls in half. Now that's what I call preventive maintenance.

We were called upon to cope with a new trend in urban construction – high-rise apartments and office buildings. This too created new problems. Tenants insisted on storing propane tanks in their lockers. People kept stealing hoses out of hall lockers to use at their cottages as fenders for their boats. Some of them sold the brass nozzles and couplings to scrap metal dealers.

The fire stations close to waterways – rivers and canals – branched out into water rescue. Their response time is incredible. In just a matter of minutes they can launch their Zodiac boats and save someone in distress. A summer doesn't go by that they aren't called out 70-75 times to pluck someone out of the water or off a disabled boat.

All of our firefighters were trained in First Aid. A Rescue Squad was born.

The treatment of hazardous materials was added to our quiver. Specialists were trained in arson detection. The HazMat guys also took their turn on the roster as regular firefighters.

More modern, sophisticated firefighting and lifesaving equipment was added to our resources. If you hoped to keep up, a strong back was no longer enough. You had to exercise that muscle we call a brain.

Some of our equipment was so old it should have been pensioned off. Fire trucks take a real beating but we try to keep them gleaming. One of the mistakes our department made was buying fire towers from Sweden at a cost of half a million dollars each. I'm no rocket scientist, but those jobbies were built for California, and not this part of the world. They were computerized cherry pickers that were supposed to operate at 135 feet in all kinds of weather. They didn't work. We had to bring them inside to thaw them out and check the computer chip. The idea was sound – pick people off balconies, but most high-rise fires are fought from the inside.

Fire In a High-Rise Hotel
(Beacon Arms Hotel)

The Code 9 call came in at 2.30 p.m. We had a working fire in a downtown high-rise hotel. There was a lot of smoke and bright flames. Some people were believed to be trapped on the upper floors.

The only thing in our favour was that it was a warm, sunny day.

The building was 22 stories high and the fire was on the eighteenth floor. We were going to earn our big salaries today.

We entered the main lobby, where alarm bells and horns were deafening. The building was loaded with smoke from the eighteenth floor up. We set up a command post in a room off the main lobby. The staff and management were helpful, providing floor plans so we could try to figure out what was burning. Luckily, the floor plans were identical for every floor except for four big penthouses at the top.

We laid our hoses into the hotel's system and began to battle our first major high-rise fire. Would we take a shitkicking? Time would tell.

Six of us boarded an elevator and got off on the sixteenth floor – two floors below the main fire floor. We were wearing air masks and they were new to us.

We checked the fire hose boxes on the sixteenth floor so we'd know where they'd be on the fire floor. It's important to know exactly where you're going in smoke, and perhaps total darkness. Hose lines are like umbilical cords to guide you back out.

We walked up two floors and pulled all the hose out of the box. If you didn't pull it out completely, the part of the hose left in the box would buck and snake when the water was turned on. We turned the nozzle to fog to get some air.

The Captain ordered a door broken down. We radioed our dispatcher that we were going to punch out windows for ventilation. The dispatcher relayed the word to the police and they cleared the sidewalk and street of people. Air currents can carry shards of glass for hundreds of yards and people can be maimed or killed.

We continued to break down doors on the eighteenth floor to check for guests and to ventilate. God, we were whacked but beginning to get the fire knocked down. The fire started in a room full of mattresses. They were the new foam filled mattresses that are so good for your lungs and health if you have to ingest their smoke. Great news!

The Captain was well pleased with our quick response. There was plenty of smoke, water and structural damage but no loss of life. At least not on the 18th floor. The pumper crew checking the main floor found an elderly little lady who worked on a switchboard near a fire door. She wouldn't leave her switchboard until she had phoned every room. The poor thing died of smoke inhalation and she still had her headset on. God rest her soul. Her name was Mary McCormick. Her son, Donny, was one of the finest Fire Chiefs I ever had the pleasure to work with.

A small Portuguese man was running around through the smoke yelling: "Mario, I can't find my son, Mario." One of the elevators was jammed shut and I had a real sick feeling we were about to find Mario. We forced the elevator door open. What a fucking horror show. A man had died a terrible death. The heat inside the elevator probably hit over 500°F. He had fouled himself and the look on his face was unbelievable. His eyes were open and full of tears. His fingernails were out of his skin, almost down to the second knuckle. Behind me, I could hear the desperate and distraught father: "Mario, please God, where is Mario?"

Two detectives entered the elevator and ordered me out. They said they were taking over. I said: "No!"

They said: "We're going to report you to your Chief."

I said: "Fuck you." I grabbed a wet cloth. Mario's dad was coming closer. I washed Mario's face and closed his eyes. The cops said: "Don't touch the body." I told them: "Fuck off." I took off my fire coat and put it over Mario. I made sure his hands were covered, his face was clean and his eyes were shut. All I could smell was smoke, shit, piss and puke.

I went back out into the corridor. Mario's dad was there.

All I could say was "I'm so sorry, your son is dead."

He fell into my arms, sobbing uncontrollably. I said to him: "Are you strong enough to identify him?"

Through his tears, he said: "Yes." There was a dim 60-watt light bulb in the elevator. I helped his father in and asked him if it was his son. He looked at him and fell to his knees. I was glad I had washed his son's face and covered his hands.

The father kissed his son. I turned the heartbroken man, who was in shock, over to an ambulance attendant. The two detectives looked on with stunned looks on their faces. The Captain didn't say anything. He just patted me on the back.

I couldn't have answered him anyway. I was crying.

At the same fire, Pat Dorion was lowered by a rope, dangling 20 floors up, and saved two American tourists from certain death. Pat Dorion was presented with the Johnny Harrison Award for bravery beyond the call of duty. I have the honour, privilege and pleasure to call him my friend.

Note: Water boils at 212° Fahrenheit. The temperature on the top floor of a high rise can reach 600 degrees during a bad fire. After 400 degrees your hair disappears in super-heated air. Next to go are your ears. They are mostly all gristle. Somewhere between 400 and 500 degrees the wax in your ears starts to boil. Just think, in the old days, we went into rooms with those temperatures and we didn't have facemasks or Scott air bottles.

Why Do Captains Have Grey Hair?

Why do Captains always have grey hair? It's part of the job description. It comes with the territory.

We were a rough, tough bunch and we were constantly in trouble or in scrapes at fires or in the station. We were gung-ho firefighters who drank too much and were hung over too often – well above the national average.

It was a lovely summer morning. We were being given our duties for the day by our wonderful, chubby, grey-haired Captain.

"Ralph, you drive the pump!"

"Captain, I should have told you. I don't get my license back for two more weeks."

"Don't worry about it. Steve, you drive the pump."

"Captain, I'm really embarrassed. I don't get my license back for another month."

"Hey, don't sweat it. Tommy, you drive."

"Sorry, Captain, I get mine back in five days."

"Jimmy?"

"Yes, Sir."

"You're junior man and you're about to learn how to drive a pump and you better have a license or I'll cut your nuts out."

"Yes, Sir, by the way, is your hair getting greyer, Captain?"

"Yes, it is, thanks to you pack of bastards. If you weren't the best pack of firefighters in the city, I'd send you all home."

"Hey, guys, he loves us, as screwed up as we are!"

He really did love us. Lung cancer took him from us in 1981.

* * * * * * * * * * *

We ran into a bad fire in a warehouse in Lowertown. I fell off a beam and should have been killed or at least ended my firefighting days handicapped, but I was lucky. All that happened was that I almost had a finger severed. Doctors were able to stitch it back on. The stitching wasn't as fancy as the embroidery you see today.

These injuries have a strange way of popping into your dreams – nightmares really. You wake up at 3 a.m. – soaking wet and hyperventilating.

* * * * * * * * * * *

We were in an old rooming house, and Tommy and I went down the stairs. I went one way and he went the other. The smoke was thick and we were wearing 30-minute Scott air packs. They're great but if you're scared, excited and pushing it, the air might only last 15 minutes.

We walked or crawled checking for victims. We opened closets and turned over furniture and beds because when children are scared they have a tendency to hide and they can fit into the smallest places.

I was working the circle in the basement area, keeping low. What a dump! Who has to live like this? I was tripping over garbage and junk and busted up furniture. I found a dresser set against a wall. I circled left with my shoulder against the wall until I found a window, which I took out with an axe to take the pressure off the room.

I stumbled into an old metal frame bed. I lifted it towards the wall but it snapped back quickly and hit me on the chest. Then I found out why. There was an unconscious, spaced out male on the bed. He was half-naked from the waist up and he had long hair down to his waist. I thought he was dead. He was in the foetal position and he had arms like legs coming out of his shoulders. He was about 5'6", weighed about 180 pounds, and was built like a brick shithouse.

I picked him up and began to carry him towards the stairs. That's when he came to. He opened his eyes and let out an ear-shattering scream. I was carrying him in my arms like a child. There was a look of terror on his face such as I had never seen before. I was trying to carry him up the narrow staircase, when he started to punch me. I was trying desperately to reach the top of the stairs so I could put him down. He reached around, tore off my facemask and began punching me in the face. I've been punched often but this time I couldn't punch back. Then he stuck his left little finger, past his second knuckle, into my left eye socket. If it had been his right hand my eye would have been forced out of the socket. I was blinded. It was so far in he was able to hook it around the inside of my skull cavity.

Finally I reached the top of the stairs. I was going crazy with pain. I couldn't see. I got him outside to the emergency vehicle and he was still flailing away at me, while I was trying to hold him down. All Hell had broken loose again when my Chief started to yell at me. He took his finger and started to stick it into my chest. He told me never to treat a member of the public like that again or "I'll send you home."

All I could see out of my left eye were shadows. The druggie took another swing at me. I blocked his punch and gave him one of my left-hook sleeping pills. The Chief was going nuts.

It was a miracle my eye wasn't gouged out. I shouldn't have nailed him because, after all, he was a taxpayer. Thankfully, I didn't lose the eye but it caused me great pain and worry about after effects. I went back to work a week and a half later. I still had a black and swollen eye. To this day, I have a torn muscle in my left eye, and the marks from the druggie's finger are still visible.

My one fear was that, with one eye, I couldn't have a "D" license to drive the pumper or aerial trucks. The Chief was so pissed off with me that he had me transferred to a station out in the boonies. I was really brassed off when I was transferred but my new Chief made me feel better when he told me the department couldn't keep all the good men uptown. But, hey, the opera ain't over until the fat lady sings. I'd be back!

Injuries and Rehab

When you're uptown and running at flank speed all the time the shift goes by quickly. I wasn't where the main action was anymore. I'd not only had a station change, I'd had a shift change as well.

I didn't know my crewmembers and they didn't know me, but there wasn't much of a lull before the first storm. The news was bad, the very worst kind. A big explosion had blown the front off a large department store. The Captain of # 3 station, Lou Martin, was leading his men in and took the main brunt of the blast. He was under tons of brick and debris, and someone had to tell his wife, Fran.

I went and got her out of Mass at St. Patrick's Basilica, a Protestant boy like me wandering through a giant Catholic church. When I caught her eye she looked like a deer caught in a car's head-lights. She knew immediately why I was there; her husband was either dead or badly injured.

We went to see him in hospital. What a mess! He still had a shard of brick stuck in the side of his right eye socket. He had two broken legs, a broken wrist and arm, four missing teeth, and needed

60 stitches. His nose was broken and he could only see us through a slit of one eye. He was semi-conscious and all drugged up. He spent three months recovering in hospital, and walked with a slight limp thereafter.

* * * * * * * * * * * *

Once I was injured at a fire and wound up in a hospital bed feeling sorry for myself. The hospital was a rehab centre 220 miles away from home. I was banged up when I fell off a beam 12-feet up and my 30-pound air tank hit me on the back of my neck. When I hit the concrete floor I should have broken my back or my neck. I stayed motionless for at least 10 minutes in case my spinal cord had been severed.

They wheeled me away to a trauma unit, laced up in a neck and back brace, and stretched out on a backboard. I was in rehab for a few months but the worst was yet to come. The City personnel department tried to terminate me because they thought I'd be incapable of carrying out the work required of a firefighter. That's gratitude. My union went to bat for me and I got my job back. God bless my union. They didn't let it happen.

While I was in rehab, I had a roommate who was in bad shape. He was fighting a fire and his ladder was blown into some hydro lines. The top wire carried 14,000 volts, and the two below carried 7,000 volts each. He was blown clear over the top wire and into a snow bank. He should have died right then and there but didn't. He told me he wished he had. He was waiting to be fitted out with artificial hands, and said it would have been better if he had flipped the other way and lost both feet instead. He said: "Jimmy, it's so demeaning to have someone wipe your ass."

When he was released he went home. His wife left him, and he committed suicide.

Severe burns, serious injuries and deaths are not included in a firefighter's job description but they come with the territory.

Nobody but firefighters and their families know what we go through physically and emotionally. You cannot but be affected by the suffering and death that is part of your job. How do you come down when you're giving mouth to mouth to a two and a half year old child who is blue and cold? You know he's dead. You know it's too late but you try anyway.

When I went home at the end of that shift, a smart-ass neighbour said: "Have a good night in the sack, Jimmy?" I blew. "No, I fucking didn't, you fucking puke. I held a two and a half year old boy in my arms. He was dead. My heart's broken, just as your fucking nose is gonna be if you say one more sarcastic word."

He apologized. We became close friends. Sometimes you have to blow your cork to put your point across.

The Unexpected

I got a phone call from an ambulance driver friend of mine. One of my brother firefighters' hands actually caught on fire. The doctors put his hands in jelly laced with antibiotics and he didn't lose them. He was burned so severely that his hands were transparent, and you could see all the bones. It was like looking at an X-Ray.

* * * * * * * * * * * *

Somebody phoned in to complain about a strange odour in a real nice neighbourhood. We sent a pump with a Captain and crew. The pump pulled up to a front door and the Captain radioed the dispatcher and told him it was a two-storey brick dwelling. There was nothing visible but we were checking it out. The Captain and two men walked up to the front door and rang the bell. An agitated 25-year-old man answered the door. "What's your problem?", he demanded rudely to the Captain. Our Captain was not the kind of man you talked to rudely – unless you wanted to find yourself on your back.

The Captain explained politely that we were checking out a complaint. The man tried to close the door but the Captain sensed something was amiss and ordered the dispatcher to send Code 10 – police wanted. Two of our men headed down the basement steps. The Captain went upstairs and other firefighters started checking the main floor.

Then it happened.

The whole place blew. There was a huge fireball. The man had been storing illegal chemicals in the basement. The occupant ran out the front door. The Captain was knocked to the floor. Firefighters on the first floor were bowled over.

The men in the basement took the full blast. Their mates walked through a wall of fire to drag them out. They lived but were grotesquely burned. The Captain never worked another fire. He felt responsible for what happened and retired. What a loss for the department!

* * * * * * * * * * *

One of the strangest calls we ever received was to a nursing home in the middle of winter. I really don't know why we were called, because when we got there a 90-year-old male resident was very dead and very cold. The police and the coroner were called in.

The coroner was demanding answers from the staff and they were standing around looking very uncomfortable. Somehow, the elderly gentleman had managed to exit by a back door at 3 a.m. It was about 30° below F. He froze to death on a park bench in the foetal position. Two staff members were afraid they'd lose their jobs so they carried the frail body inside and put it back in bed. Rigor mortis had set in so they broke damned near every one of his brittle bones, trying to straighten out the body. The nursing home didn't want publicity and settled out of court. The two attendants were given pink slips.

* * * * * * * * * * *

We had a working fire on our hands at 2 a.m. – lots of smoke and open flames. It was way below Zero and the streets and sidewalks were very slippery. It was a chemical warehouse fire and already through the roof. It was going to be a long night.

Captain Fern Gervais jumped down from the pump, went ass over teakettle, and broke his leg in seven places. What a mess! He hit an ice patch and his leg just shattered. His fire fighting days were over. He was lucky he didn't lose the leg.

We were ignorant of the toxic danger of some of the new chemical fumes that were coming out of the warehouse. We started to barf, and one fireman collapsed. Three of us were rushed to hospital.

A doctor came in and told us we were crazy to do what we did for a living. He said that according to our blood work we were all dead. That wasn't the first time a doctor told me I was dead. But, hey, that's what we got paid the big bucks for.

We Stand On Guard For Thee

Every city gets a good return for their money from the fire department. The public gets 24-hour, seven days a week service. If, at a Chief's discretion, you are needed for a major fire you can be called back in for duty.

Many times the phone would ring to inform me I was needed. It was no picnic being rousted from a warm sleep at 2 a.m. in below Zero temperatures. You knew that a big one was rolling somewhere. The dispatcher wasn't calling to invite you to a marshmallow roast.

Why do all major fires have to happen around 2 a.m.? Water cannons were shooting water out at the rate of 1,000 gallons a minute. What a mess! Four firefighters were unaccounted for. There was lots of screaming and crying. I ended up crawling through rubble and broken glass looking and listening. I could see part of a fire coat and started to dig with my hands. We didn't want to use shovels, axes or picks because we didn't want to further injure a buried victim.

We pulled at the fire coat and dug around him. He was badly hurt and barely breathing. Both of his shoulders were pulled out of their sockets and he was in excruciating pain. We couldn't get the beam off his legs. Finally, between us, we got him out, onto a stretcher, and he was taken to hospital. Still one man was missing. We were all crawling in different directions. I inched towards a beam and worked my way around it. I could see a piece of a fire coat and fire boots. His legs were almost severed. How do you lift a ton of steel off a fire-fighter's legs? I yelled for help and started to sob. I couldn't help it. We worked around his body gingerly. His eyes were wide open. They reflected a combination of pain, fear and sadness. Both his legs were badly broken, maybe in six or seven places. God, my heart was breaking. I could hear it cracking. The police arrived and tried to move us out. I told them he was my friend and that I knew his brother. I asked them to call him to come and identify the body.

I closed his eyes and started to clean his face. A detective told me not to touch the body. It was now a crime scene. Here we go again.

"Fuck you!"

I kept on washing Johnny Harrison's face. I kept on cleaning off the soot and smoke. The detective came at me again. He said it was their job now and told me to leave the body alone.

I called my Chief, Tony McCarthy, and Lieutenant Fitzpatrick over and told them I needed their help. I told the Chief I didn't want Johnny's brother to identify the body looking as it did so I was cleaning him up. The Chief, looking at the detective, said it sounded like a kind thing to do. I took my fire coat off and covered him with it. His brother came to identify him. What a night!

Looking back, I was rude with the detectives. Things were said in anger both ways. It wasn't a lack of respect for police. Three of my brothers were police officers. I'm the first to admit that relationships and respect have improved immensely over the years.

* * * * * * * * * * *

When I was in a rehabilitation hospital, a young firefighter from another city was brought in. He had tried to extricate a driver from a transport truck, who was unconscious and bleeding badly. The firefighter got in the cab with him and that's when all Hell broke loose. The gas tanks let go and the driver was burned to a crisp. The firefighter was pulled out by his legs, but not before his hair, ears and face were badly burned. The doctors took skin from his legs and thighs and grafted it onto his head.

My God. Was he in pain! But his worst pain was yet to come. His wife came to visit him and left in shock. She wouldn't even let their children see him. Let's face it. Physical pain is just pain. It goes away. But there's no pain like a broken heart.

* * * * * * * * * * *

Another time we were fighting a bad fire at a pharmaceutical company. One of my mates broke a leg and almost lost it. His doctor told him there was no way he could go back to work. The only option left to him was to join the Fire Prevention Bureau.

How did I come to terms with grief and suffering and death? To be honest, I never did reconcile myself to tragedy. I never did become blasé and hardboiled about death. The loss of a brother firefighter or a fire victim hit me hard each and every time.

There were times I was traumatized and didn't even know it. I'd go out and get drunk. When you picked up somebody's head after a bad auto accident the only thing that numbed your jangling nerves was drink. My main poison was beer, and I could never understand why anyone would want to buy a measly six-pack. I never knew why they bothered to make six-packs in the first place.

I was sick of being tired and tired of being sick. I was tired of hurting others as well as myself. The only time I ever hurt anyone was when I was drinking. The first time I went for help in the early 1970s, the alcohol addiction research doctor told me he didn't think I should quit without something to calm me down. He gave me fifty #10 Valium pills and told me to come back when I needed more. I ate them like peanuts. I was walking around spaced half the time – but I was sober.

When I went back all he would ask me was "Are you calmer now?" The only way I could have been calmer was if he'd taken out my spine. Years later a good friend told me that the British Medical Journal reported that some of the shit I was swallowing was more dangerous than heroin and much more addictive. The dummy that was treating me told me I'd have to take 50 mg a day for 50 years before I'd become addicted.

One of the reasons I survived is that I allowed myself to cry. My father always told me there is nothing wrong with crying. It's not a female thing or a male thing, it's just a thing you do. If something is affecting or bothering you – CRY. Get it out because you will feel better.

Many of my brother firefighters never did learn how to cry. They washed away their nightmares with different tears – tears they thought were at the bottom of the bottle. I was no different. I tried that too, but the bottle only provided temporary escape from the devils within.

I'm a loner. When I quit drinking with the help of Alcoholics Anonymous, I was like the kid on the block who had nobody to play with. I didn't fit in. I didn't fish, hunt, bowl, curl or hang out in taverns.

New Equipment

The two most significant advances in firefighting in the 20th century happened on my watch. The first was SCBA (Self

Contained Breathing Apparatus), and I don't know how we ever managed without this equipment.

It's a marvel that more of us didn't die from the chemicals we ingested. We swallowed a lot of smoke before air bottles and air masks became standard issue.

The second innovation was the Jaws of Life. A set of Jaws is worth about $27,000 today, but our political masters are always penny-wise and pound-foolish. We didn't have money in our budgets to buy them. There's no way of knowing how many lives have been saved by the Jaws of Life. They were developed as a rescue tool for racecar tracks.

The Jaws of Life are four feet high. They remind me of the robot C3P0 in Star Wars. What they can't do in an emergency is not worth mentioning. The Jaws can cut, spread or ram. They can snap a car doorpost like a matchstick in a couple of seconds. They can cut through a steering column like it was a Tootsie Roll. The Jaws can open 32 inches wide and they have a pulling and cutting force of between eight and eleven tons – depending on the model, and it does all this using only one quart of hydraulic fluid. The fluid is fire resistant, electrically non-conductive and environmentally friendly.

A firefighter can take a roof off a car in a matter of seconds, and we practiced with the Jaws cutting up cars in wrecking yards. Using the Jaws of Life is like cutting through a tin can. Unfortunately, the City didn't want to buy us this equipment. It was left to the Canadian Legion to come up with the money. God Bless the veterans!

Also of importance to firefighting was the introduction of pumper trucks. The pumper takes a trickle of water from a hydrant and turns it into a high-pressure jet that can bowl a man off his feet.

Shift Work

I remember being in a line-up in a grocery store one day and talking to a man behind me. He made some crack about "spending your life in bed". He thought that all we did was eat lumberjack meals in the fire station and sleep the rest of the time. He was like my neighbour who gave me the same shot, in jest, every time we met on the street.

I was weary of his broken record comments, but they say he who is slow to anger is greater than the Mighty. I kept my temper in check and said nothing.

My neighbour had every reason to think we were lead swingers because we only worked 13 days a month and had up to six consecutive days off. When I joined the Department we worked a 56-hour workweek for $3,600 a year.

We had little down time however, while at work. When we weren't out on fire or medical calls we performed maintenance on vehicles and gauges, cleaned up pumpers, aerials and ladders, as well as the kitchen, bathrooms and floors. There are no cleaning ladies in fire stations. Then we attended lectures or studied manuals. The mind is a great computer but you have to fuel it.

Nowadays, firefighters work a screwball 42-hour week. One of my shifts was 10 hours a day Mondays to Thursdays and then six days off. Or, I was called on to work 14 hours a day Thursdays to Saturdays and then I'd have five days off.

The killer was one 24-hour shift a month. We'd be at the fire station from 7 a.m. one day to 7 a.m. the next day. There was always something to do but, when all the work was done, we could catch forty winks. They were hardly quality naps because you were always listening for the alarm. After a 24-hour shift, we'd work three 14-hour nights. We couldn't leave the station even when it was quiet, so we do our own shopping and eat in. If you see a fire truck at a shopping plaza buying groceries it isn't because the firefighters are too cheap to use their own cars. It's because they're on duty, and if a fire call comes in, they could be dispatched to the scene from the shopping plaza parking lot.

On Sundays when we pulled the 24-hour shift we'd really go whole hog – spaghetti and meatballs for lunch and a roast for dinner. We joked that Sunday was "Calorie Day". Everybody pitched in to prepare the meals. More often than not, a call came in just when we were ready to eat. Yes, firefighters do eat well, but they pay for their own groceries, cook their own meals, and in the early years of the department, we even had to buy our own stoves and fridges.

Back in the early 1960s, one cheap fireman didn't like chipping in for meals. When nobody was looking he would get into the pot of leftover spaghetti sauce. One day, before we sacked out, we loaded up the sauce with hot chili peppers – anything hot we would lay our hands on. Sure enough, he started warming it up and cooking himself a free meal. That afternoon he thought he might have to go to hospital to have his stomach pumped out. When he went for a dump he just about had to tie himself down on the toilet seat. It looked good on the cheap prick!

I wish I could make wise guys see some of the horrible things I've had to witness in my life as a firefighter. They think all firefighters do is play checkers. I have never seen a checkerboard in a fire station. I've never seen a Dalmatian either. Those long shifts are cruel and unusual punishment for even a dog.

I have never considered myself the sharpest pin in the cushion. I made it through high school and played four years of offensive and defensive football. Yes, I wore a helmet and didn't take too many hits on the head.

My dream was to be a firefighter. I took on tough, dirty jobs to build up my strength. I worked on a pipeline. I washed dishes and peeled potatoes. The most demanding physical job I had was on a garbage truck. When I started I could barely, with difficulty, wrestle one can out to the packer. Not long after, I could walk out to the truck with a can in each hand, keeping them off the ground about two inches – two cans – great for the shoulder muscles.

Firefighters earn every penny they're paid. It's unfortunate that some people have to learn this the hard way – like having a fire in their own house, losing a loved one to fire, or being badly injured in a car accident and having to be extricated from a wreck with the Jaws of Life.

My wonderful wife, Sharon, suffered along with me. I can't count on the fingers of both hands the times I scared the heck out of her – wondering if I'd come home all bloody or burned, or if she'd be picked up by the Fire Department Chief's car and rushed to hospital, not knowing if I was injured, critical or dead.

Sharon says she thanked God every day I got out with my life, because there were more times than not that she didn't think I would.

A Gallon Of Water Weighs 10 Pounds

Terry was a little guy but he was all tiger meat. He was one of the great firefighters and he had all three of the major qualifications needed – guts, strength and a sharp mind.

In the 1960's you had to be 5'8" tall and weigh a minimum of 150 pounds. Terry was just over 5'7" and weighed 140 pounds soaking wet. He wanted to be a firefighter so badly he could taste it. He wanted a job he knew he could do and be respected doing it.

I asked him: "Terry, how good are your kidneys?"

He said: "What?"

I told him that during a drill period the Captain told us we had to be careful putting water into a building, especially if the floor was over men working below, because of the weight. With modern pumps and aerials and the right nozzle you can deliver tons of water.

"What the hell has that got to do with my kidneys, Jimmy?"

I told him the Captain said that a gallon of water weighs 10 pounds.

"When you go for your physical, just before you go into the examining room, get to the nearest washroom and drink a gallon of water. Then go in and get weighed. Put lifts in your socks to make yourself taller."

I thought he was going to kiss me.

"You son of a bitch. I'll practice."

Two weeks later I drove him to the doctor who did fire department physicals. He was a crusty old fellow left over from the Second World War who had seen it all. He did amputations in the field during the war, and helped a lot of soldiers survive. He was a great doctor but had absolutely no bedside manner.

Terry went to the washroom and force-fed himself a whole gallon of water. He damn near barfed, but it worked. The nurse, another crusty old specimen, told him to strip and get on the scale.

Terry stripped down to his socks and got on the scale. He weighed in at just over 151 pounds. He was in unbelievable pain. The lifts in his socks worked, too. The nurse wrote down 5' 8" and a fraction. Was he pleased but what pain!

The doctor came in to check him for hernias and stuck his fingers around Terry's crown jewels. The pressure from the old doctor's rough hands damned near made him piss all over him. The doctor examined his body and asked: "Who the fuck took out your appendix?" The water in Terry's stomach made the appendix scar stick out like a pair of lips.

Terry answered him: "You did, doctor."

"Good job, good job. Looks like you got yourself a job on the fire department, son."

Terry's back teeth were floating. He left the examining room and pissed for 15 minutes. Then he bought me beer – lots of beer. He was one happy camper.

Do As You're Told

Code 9 means a working fire. Code 9 means certain automatics.

When Code 9 is activated, a pumper, a back-up pump, an aerial, a rescue vehicle and an emergency car are deployed. A Code

5 or a possible Code 5 means loss of life. We wheeled along a downtown street. You could see the fire and smoke. Patio doors were open and burning drapes were flapping in the wind. The drapes were blowing straight out. I was an acting Lieutenant on the aerial. I was fairly new to command but I was trained by the very best so I had to be good. I counted the floors in the old high-rise. The fire was on the 8th. I told my driver to pull into the parking lot. He argued: "But the Chief wants us at the front."

"Screw the Chief. This is not a textbook fire. The fire's at the back. That's where we're setting up. Put the aerial up on the eighth floor balcony."

"BUT THE CHIEF…"

"Screw the Chief!"

"It won't reach," he said.

"Yes it will. Do as you're fucking told."

There was lots more screaming and yelling but the aerial went straight up, fully extended, and reached over the balcony rails.

My driver obviously didn't understand that a fire station is not a democracy, and neither is a fire scene. A good officer thinks for everyone. Orders are followed and discussed later. There is no time for debate when a fire is humping. Firefighters belong to a Para-military organization. They're trained to respond instantly to a command, and there's no room for argument. They obey orders and question them afterwards. Take discipline away and you also take away respect. Their lives and the lives of their fellow firefighters might just hang on responding to a command instantly, instinctively and without question. Commands are not given because an officer has a parade square complex. They are given because, in his best judgement, they're the instructions that will work best.

Your men become extensions of your body. We become one. A building is just a building and a car is just a car but a living fire-fighter is priceless.

Donny, Get An Air Mask

"Donny, get an air mask and follow me."

"You bet."

Donny and I climbed the almost straight up aerial ladder in wind and rain. It would be scary for anyone but, hey, that's what we get paid for. I stepped off the aerial and got my feet on the balcony eight floors up. I helped Donny off the end of the aerial. Before he could say it to me, I said it to him: "I'm scared, too!"

He probably already knew that from the look on my face. He was new on the job and 10 years younger than me.

"This is where the fun begins. We're going in."

We had a one and a half-inch hose line with a full fog nozzle. "Stick to me like shit to a blanket, Donny. If I turn around I want to be able to touch you."

You learn. You pass it on. You learn to keep close to the floor. You might find a child or an unconscious person on the floor. Find a window. Take it out with an axe or a chair to get some air and clear the room.

"You won't be able to see across the room, so put your hand through the back of my belt. Stick close to me. Understand?"

"You bet!"

Donny and I were close friends, and he was relaxed with me. We entered a room that looked like a paint factory after an explosion. There was plastic in every colour of the spectrum. We had all the ingredients for a chemical blaze.

Donny said: "What the fuck is burning?"

I stepped on what I thought was a mattress. It was the chest of a very badly burned and very dead 300-pound male. An empty liquor bottle was nearby. When I stepped on him, both of his eyeballs left their sockets. It wasn't a pretty sight.

Donny hurled in his mask.

The apartment was full of plastic furniture and we had a quasi-chemical fire on our hands.

Donny started to choke on his up-chuck. I told him to calm down.

"We are going to buddy breathe with my mask. Take your mask off now." Our air bottles had air enough for 30 minutes but when your adrenaline is pumping and you're moving fast and exerting yourself you can cut that down to 15-18 minutes of air.

Donny removed his mask. He had trained in drill school for an emergency like this. I told him: "We have the fire knocked down. We're going out the front door of the apartment and down the hall to the internal fire escapes. Do you understand? Let's do it!"

"Yes, Sir."

We took turns getting breaths of air from my facemask. It was no picnic breathing in the same mask with the smell of Donny's vomit, but the only choice we had was bad breath or death. It was weird! That song *He's Not Heavy, He's My Brother* kept running through my mind.

We made it to the stairwell, but not before taking a shit kicking. We both ended up in hospital.

That's when I first saw the doctor with the quizzical look on his face.

"How's Donny?"

"He's going to be OK," the doctor said. "I have to X-Ray your lungs again. I couldn't get a picture. I have the results of your blood work. I thought I was working on an autopsy. The hair is burned out of your nose and the fibres are burned from the top third of your lungs because you ingested so much polyvinyl chloride. You and Donny both should be dead."

Donny died early in 1996. He was only 46. I had four cancer scares myself two years later. At least, I thought they were cancer scares. When a doctor told me all the "fur" had been burned from my nose and lungs, it was as a result of inhaling noxious fumes from plastics and other synthetics. Eventually, globules of plastic worked out of my body and formed lumps on the back of my head. When one lump was lanced, an oval piece of plastic, half the size of a marble, popped out. Was it worth it? I know I speak for Donny, too, when I answer "YES".

There were other times I couldn't answer YES. We answered an emergency call. A local college professor had suffered a heart attack. I was doing the very best I knew how to revive him – chest compression and resuscitation. When I was beginning mouth to mouth, he suddenly lunged forward and broke two of my front teeth. The professor had a brand new disease. He was one-in-a-million. He had AIDS. I checked out fine but it was very scary.

That wasn't our only brush with AIDS. Years later, we answered a Code 1025 – Person Down. The victim was a 27-year-old drug dealer. There was blood all over the place.

We didn't know he'd been stabbed in the heart with an ice pick. One of my young men began mouth-to-mouth resuscitation and heart massage. The blood from his pierced heart shot out in a jet and hit him in the face and eyes.

The victim had AIDS and was in the final stages. My firefighter was rushed to hospital immediately and washed down from the insides of his eye sockets out, to the insides of his nose and ears. Was he frightened? You bet!

As a precaution he was not allowed to have conjugal relations with his wife for 90 days.

Code 9 – Working Fire

3.51 a.m.

Things can go wrong very quickly on the fire ground. You ready yourself to expect the unexpected. Fires are like snow flakes. No two are the same.

We had another Code 9 in Centretown, and again, people were trapped. The nearest fire hydrant was 200 yards away and frozen stiff. We were ready to roll but we had no water.

The temperature was 27 below and a brisk north wind was blowing. This was old-fashioned firefighting at its very worst. We had no air masks or Scott air packs.

It was get in, stay low, and take your beating. I was a rookie with a seasoned crew of World War 11 veterans. As far as I was concerned, those guys could walk on water. My God, I loved those guys. They never had to worry about dying and going to Hell because they'd already been there and back during the war.

The Captain yelled to the ladder crew to punch a hole in the roof so we could ventilate the house. I could hear the sirens of more fire trucks coming, and then the sounds of children crying and screaming.

For a split second, you ask yourself: "What am I doing on a job like this?" There is no answer, I guess, except maybe I was a couple of sandwiches short of a picnic.

We broke in the front door. A child's lifeless body is handed out and the circle begins. Please, please, God, no more! But it's not our night. We fight our way up the stairs, and find two more children in a back room – dead from smoke inhalation. We circle, checking each room, tipping over beds, reaching into closets, hoping and praying, please, God, no more.

We stick our heads out an upstairs window for a wonderful breath of fresh air, but the acrid smoke is being blown back in our faces. You upchuck your groceries. My God, what a job!

We enter the main bedroom and tip a bed over. There's nobody under it. Then instinct clicks in and I open a closet door. A mother and child are in the closet. Her eyes are wide open and she has the most God-awful look of fear on her face. She's trying to do what a mother does best – take care of her children. My heart contracts. I hear a faint sound and move through the darkness towards it. I feel the warm flesh and almost lifeless body of a small child. Please, God, let some good come out of this horror show. I pick the child up. She's almost gone. I put my mouth over her mouth and nose to get a good seal. I can taste smoke and snot, but it's working. She coughs and pukes and I clean her mouth so she can breathe on her own.

We retreat to the station to lick our wounds and vent our frustrations. The count is five dead and one in hospital. Word comes down from the Chief's office that the little girl will live. I'm so happy. Being a firefighter means your emotions go up and down like a whore's drawers on pay night.

* * * * * * * * * * *

Another emergency call in the middle of the night. It was 4:30 a.m. We got a medical call for a wino who was holed up in a fleabag of a rooming house with a case of cheap red wine. He just stayed in bed and fouled himself from every orifice of his body. What a mess! We stabilized him and waited for the ambulance.

Gentleman that I am, I told the ambulance attendants that the guy was pretty high from every dimension and asked them if they wanted to borrow a couple of air masks.

Their answer was "Don't tell us how to do our jobs and we won't tell you how to do yours. OK?"

So we bade them goodbye. Soon after I heard a window being broken on the second floor where the drunk was. The two ambulance attendants were barfing and retching. One of them called down: "Hey, Mac, can we borrow those air masks?"

Our answer? "Fuck you" – and we returned to the fire station.

* * * * * * * * * * *

There's just enough time to grab a coffee and put the hoses in the tower to dry before the next call comes in. At first, it looks like nothing. We do a quick outside check and then notice the basement is full of smoke. The Captain orders me to check it out. I take a one and a half-inch hose to act as my umbilical cord. If you get lost in the smoke, the hose is your way out. The front door of the TV & Appliances store is smashed in and I enter with my hose line. I'm looking for the seed of the fire. It's blacker than pitch in the basement. My sixth sense kicks into over-drive. Danger!

I'm about 15 feet from the bottom of the stairs when it happens. The explosion lights up the whole basement for a fraction of a second, and then there is total darkness again. My metal helmet is blown from my head – never to be seen again. I'm in pain so I know I'm not dead, unless I'm in Hell and on the hot coals. All of a sudden there's screaming and I realize it's coming from me. I'm under a stove and fridge and other debris. I'm crying like a baby and terrified. I don't want to die. I can't see my hand in front of my face, but I hear my heart pounding. Next comes the sound of glass breaking and I can see a hand light shining through the thick acrid smoke and dust. I push, pull and crawl out from under the fridge and stove. Slowly, I work my way towards the light. Then I hear another sound – that of my built-in alarm bells telling me I have three minutes of air left.

I'm 25 years old, and sure as hell don't want to die. The alarm bells stop and my face piece collapses against my face. I'm out of air. The lights I see give me a rough idea of where the basement stairs are. I take off my facemask and put my head down a few inches from the floor. All I get is a full breath of filthy toxic air. I puke again and again. I'm losing consciousness at the bottom of the stairs when two of my firefighting brothers grab me and drag me up the stairs. I step outside, take a couple of breaths of God's air and collapse. I wake up in hospital and the first person I see is my girl-friend and future wife, Sharon. She's either a vision, an Angel or she's real. She's real. I'm ALIVE!

* * * * * * * * * * *

Code 9. Another working fire. My God, look at the sky! You could see it a mile away. What the fuck was burning? It was a shopping mall and the fire was going good. Flames were shooting through the roof. The first hydrant we tried wasn't working because somebody had taken the caps off and shoved rags and other debris down it.

It was going to be a long night, but at least it was an outside fire with no loss of life. A few hours later a cop came by and told us they had a puke in custody for deliberately setting the blaze.

This guy went into a bar about 10 blocks away reeking of gasoline. He told the arson squad that the owner of the mall had paid him $1,000 to torch it. He bought 10 gallons of gas. The dumb fucker didn't know that a quart of gasoline, used properly, has the explosive capacity of four sticks of dynamite. He poured the whole 10 gallons around the back of the mall and lit it. It blew him down the hill. He shit himself and pissed his pants. He thought he was going to die. He ran until he saw a place to get a drink to calm his nerves, not realizing how he smelled of gas and shit. Oh, well, another dirtbag off to jail! Good!

* * * * * * * * * * *

It was mid-afternoon, and there was plenty of smoke, and only a pumper at the fire scene. It's hard to fight a fire without a ladder or a rescue crew. Firefighting is not an exact science. If you don't have a ladder crew to open the roof and conditions are wrong, you can end up getting a back draft that will put you on somebody's lawn across the street. Sometimes we didn't realize the dangers facing us.

We broke down the front door. You couldn't see your hand in front of your face. We were scared and apprehensive. The house was hot and fully loaded. We had to make it to the stairs and get some windows open or this place would blow.

We got to the top of the stairs. It was well over 400 degrees and the smoke was Technicolor because of the different things burning. We got an axe blade through a window and the smoke poured out.

We started the circle, checking every room, and found no victims.

Sometimes, homeowners will call us "rotten bastards" because we chopped up their house. This isn't true! People, especially little kids, can't be replaced. Doors and windows can.

We make a mess of interiors but, fuck it, the feeling of finding someone alive can't be described. It's the greatest rush a firefighter can have.

The Chief arrived at the same time as the ladder crew. The officer in charge of the ladder tried to impress the Chief by barking out orders to get the place ventilated. I yelled from upstairs that we had already done so.

He yelled back: "You didn't do a very good job."

Shawn screamed back down: "You brown-nosing bastard, we did a great job. Come on upstairs and I'll put this fucking axe in the side of your head."

I thought the crusty old Chief was going to piss his pants, he was laughing so hard. Shawn and I thought we were going to be charged but feelings run hot at a fire, too.

* * * * * * * * * * *

Another Code 9 – working fire – people trapped. Fresh snow was falling. We turned a corner and there were people out in the street – crying, screaming and bleeding. Two 50-year old ladies were on the lawn in a snow bank, all curled up in the foetal position. There were lots of broken bones and plenty of blood in the snow.

When a fire is really humping, you have decisions to make. If there are people inside you have to go in. Once a fire gets rolling it's all over in four or five minutes.

We busted our asses to make it upstairs. Our circle was almost complete except for one last room, where we found a sweet little old lady dead on the floor. Her housecoat was half on and half off. We could see her footprints in the fresh snow where she had made it out the window and part way down the fire escape. I guess modesty forced her to turn back to put her housecoat on. I was heartbroken.

God rest her soul.

* * * * * * * * * * *

Was winter ever going to end? A cold north wind was tearing at our fire coats and faces, and even the hydro wires were crackling in the chill. Just like us, the hydrants were frozen. It was great weather for another Code 9.

When we arrived on the scene, the heat was so intense the glass in the aluminium front door was running like water. Flames were everywhere and people were screaming. We ran up against a language barrier.

A woman had jumped from an upper storey, and she was on the lawn in the snow with a badly broken leg. Her shinbone was sticking out through her nightgown. Lots of blood and tears.

She was crying, screaming and speaking a language I couldn't understand. She was in obvious shock but the word "bambino" came out in her jumble of words. The building was laddered so we went in. I started up the stairs.

There was a little boy on the stairwell. His eyes were open, and he seemed to be looking straight at me. I took off my fire coat, wrapped him up in it, and started to cry.

I carried the little boy outside, and sat under a tree with him, not even feeling the cold. Warner Bradley came over to talk to me. He said: "Jimmy, you know he's dead, eh?"

"Yes, I know", I answered. "I couldn't get to him in time."

Warner said: "It's not your fault."

The coroner, Dr. Tom Kendall, arrived. I surrendered the child to him. He had just been on the scene at another fatality. A 74-year old man had put a double-barrelled shotgun in his mouth. Tom Kendall cried, too.

We went back to the station and I washed away chunks of burned skin that had stuck to the inside of my fire coat. I hung it in the tower to dry.

Life is so precious and yet so fragile.

Little Italy

Code 9 – another working fire, and yet again, people were believed to be trapped inside. It was a bright, sunny, fairly warm Saturday afternoon, with the temperature hovering around 65°F. The dispatcher yelled: "We're getting lots of calls on this one."

We headed east off Preston street and up a cul-de-sac. There was so much smoke you could barely see the dead end street sign. The Captain roared over his radio: "Send a back-up pump and aerial, the rescue crew, some ambulances and the police for traffic."

The place was an inferno. You're not supposed to swear but sometime sentences like "is this place ever fucking going" slipped out. The pumper laid two lines of two and a half inch hoses and boy, did we have a working fire! It was in a poor Italian neighbour-hood, where people are the salt of the earth and supposed to love one another.

An elderly woman was screaming at me in broken English: "It's my daughter's house. She was fighting with her drunken husband and he kicked a space heater down the stairs."

"Any children?" I yelled back.

"Six", she answered.

I think I said, "Fuck".

"Go in" was the command from the Captain as the Chief's car pulled up. My God, it was hot! Oil from the space heater was all over the floor. Flames and smoke were every colour of the rainbow and we hunkered down low. You could smell what firefighters get to know – the smell of death.

The drunken father was out on the front lawn giving orders to the Chief and everyone else. I wanted to kick the shit out of him so badly.

Three of the children were at the back of the house – all dead. Where were the rest? One of our men, Leo Bowes, was on a ladder leading to a second storey window. The acrid smoke pouring out was unbelievably hot. He reached through the opening and felt something. It was a child's arm. He pulled on the arm and the child came flying out the window.

He was sobbing and scared, but only slightly burned. Leo dropped the child, who broke his arm, but thankfully, he was alive.

The hunt for the mother and the other child began. We found her and her two-year-old son dead under the stairs. The coroner arrived. Tom Kendall was a crusty, no nonsense doctor.

The mother was eight months pregnant, and when we moved her body for him to examine, her foetus fell out of her horribly burned stomach. It was like watching a charred roast fall.

The hard-boiled coroner began to cry. Coroners come face to face with death almost every day and are not expected to cry. He did.

The drunken bastard shit of a husband was still weaving around screaming orders. God, I wanted a piece of that fuck.

He got off scot-free. He was never charged with anything, even though he was responsible for killing almost his entire family.

* * * * * * * * * * *

No sooner did we get back to the fire station than we were dispatched on a medical call and fire combination. Holy shit! What now? There was lots of smoke in the cancer ward at a city hospital. What the hell have we got? The smoke was dense as we entered the fourth floor. Such a different call. The sound of interior alarms was deafening, and very eerie. We took our beating and knocked out some windows for ventilation.

Then we saw it – flames and smoke coming out from under a bathroom door, accompanied by the distinctive smell of death.

The Horseman had come and gone by the time we arrived.

The Captain radioed our dispatcher: "We have a Code 5. We think it's a male but we're not sure." Basically, there was nothing left.

A 72-year old male had just had a cancer-riddled lung removed. He was wearing oxygen hooks in his nose. He had a tracheotomy from throat cancer. Somehow, he got hold of a cigarette, sneaked into the bathroom, stuck the cigarette in the hole in his throat, lit a match and disappeared. Oxygen doesn't burn but does it ever support combustion. Makes one think about quitting smoking.

* * * * * * * * * * *

2.20 a.m.

It was early spring, cool and drizzling. Spring smells so good in a gentle rain.

Our Captain said we had a working fire and "Watch your asses." There had been an explosion. We turned the corner and saw a lot of dust but no sign of flames. Our Captain told the dispatcher he needed more information. The dispatcher replied that all he knew was that someone called in an explosion and fire.

Suddenly, there she was. She wasn't a pretty sight – a 250-pound naked woman screaming and running down the street. Her eyes were out like organ stops. We ran after her. I never saw a chubbette run as fast as her before.

We caught up to her and put her in the "gut" wagon (slang for emergency car). We put blankets around her and tried to calm her down and get some information.

She was in shock. You have to be extra careful with shock victims, as you might lose them if they go into cardiac arrest. We calmed her down and looked for the source of the explosion. Her rear end and the back of her legs were bleeding and there were lots of white chunks sticking out of her ass. We put her on her stomach and applied about ten compression bandages to her wounds.

Finally, she spoke: "I will never fucking smoke again."

I asked her: "What the hell happened?"

She said she got up to take a leak after drinking lots of beer. She was sitting on the toilet smoking and threw the lighted cigarette down between her legs. Her house was at the bottom of a hill on Perkins Avenue and methane gas from other sewer systems had seeped into her house.

Then, POW, the toilet bowl blew into a hundred pieces. The explosion burned the fur completely off her pussy. Now there's one lady who won't ever bore company around the dinner table with the story of her accident.

* * * * * * * * * * *

We just got back to the station and didn't even have time to get our outerwear off. The call was a medical request for ambulance assist. It was a female, possible 10-25, and that means crazy. We took the elevator to the nineteenth floor of a high-rise building. The problem was on the twentieth floor but firefighters never get off an elevator on the problem floor for any reason. We always get off a floor or two below in case smoke or gases are present.

We walked up one flight, using the fire stairs. The screaming was deafening. It was 5.30 a.m. and people on the twentieth floor were too frightened to venture into the hallway to see what the problem was or what all the screaming was about. We get paid to do that shit.

What a sight! There was a Playboy beauty with a knockout figure and she was starkers. I took off my fire coat, put it around her, and asked what the problem was. Finally, after a few minutes, she managed to stammer out: "In there, in there". We entered her apartment and looked around, but didn't see anything, so we went back out in the hallway.

She was still shivering like a dog shitting razor blades and she had pissed on my fire coat. I didn't have to be Sherlock Holmes to deduce that because I could smell her piss and there was a puddle at her feet.

"Look, lady, I need more information. I can't find any problem. Can you help me, please?"

The problem was that a biker gang had an apartment three floors below. Their pet mascot was a nine-foot python. Somehow, it got out of its cage and into the building's plumbing system. I guess it was wandering through the pipes eating mice, rats or cats or whatever pythons eat. The bikers never reported it AWOL. Maybe they thought it would die.

The lovely lady got out of bed to get ready to go to work. She was going to take a leak when the snake came out right between her legs. I'll tell you she didn't need a laxative for a long time after that. The Humane Society came calling for the reptile. I wish they cleaned fire coats, too.

Chalk up another weird call. My wife, Sharon, knew better than to ask how my shift went when I came home. We made house calls for any number of medical reasons. We were called to put out grass fires; we put out fires in houses, apartment buildings, office buildings and shopping plazas. We rescued people and pets – any number of exotic animals – cats, dogs, budgies, parrots, monkeys and boa constrictors. I've never had to do it but I know some fire-fighters who gave the Kiss of Life to cats, dogs and birds. I'd have to draw the line with boa constrictors. There is no way I'd trust my lips to one of those suckers.

* * * * * * * * * * *

Next, we responded to a Code 7. There was a smell of gas on the lower floors of a high rise. These are the scary calls as you never know what you might have on your hands. We arrived at the building. Alarms were ringing but nobody was leaving. It was an old 12-storey complex and they'd had so many false alarms that the people who lived there ignored them. This could turn into a bad one with bodies piled up like cordwood.

This was a strange call, as there was a definite smell of gas, but it wasn't natural gas. It smelled like raw automotive gasoline.

Extra fire companies were called to help evacuate the building. Even then, people didn't want to leave. Some were in various stages of undress and others were right out of it on drugs or alcohol.

The police arrived and then people began to listen. Fear of being charged and jailed is very persuasive. The public loves fire-fighters but they don't always listen to us. Police – they're another kettle of fish. A surprising number of people don't want their names run through a computer looking for outstanding warrants.

We began a systematic search – floor by floor – trying to locate the source of the gas smell. It was strongest in the basement. The Captain pounded on doors but the occupants didn't want to answer. He pounded on one door and we found our source. A drunk opened his door and said: "What the fuck do you want, asshole?"

What a winner this puke was. He was about 40 years old, covered with tattoos and he had a week's growth of beard. He had a cigarette in his nicotine stained fingers, and there was a small light at the far end of his apartment. You could see a blue pilot light on his stove and there it was – a 50-gallon drum of gasoline standing beside a gas stove!

"You're a fucking idiot", I said to him. "What's that doing in your apartment?" His answer was "It's only gas, man. What's the big deal? It's only gas."

How did a 50-gallon drum of gas get there? He was a biker and at night he crawled out his basement window and siphoned a couple of gallons of gas from cars in the parking lot. If the air and gas mixture had been right, we could have lost the building and 100 people.

If that drum had blown, I and my fellow firefighters would have been part of the wallpaper pattern.

* * * * * * * * * * *

After 10 p.m., we could wear our ordinary street clothes at the fire station. I was wearing my nightlines and a Superman T-Shirt. Two hookers walked by and one said to the other: "Hey, look at that, a fat Superman."

Too good to last. We were called out on another fire call. It was a robbery. The robber had some sticks of dynamite strapped to him, and obviously, he couldn't read. When he bought the dynamite fuse he purchased the stuff that burned in seconds – not minutes. He had a lighter and he kept flicking his Bic. Then he disappeared. There was nothing left of him but we did find a tattoo off his arm pasted to a car a block away.

Then we had one of the weirdest calls in my entire career. A guy committed suicide and he used an electric hand drill. There were three holes in his head and three streams of blood were trickling down his face. I guess he didn't hit a critical spot until the third try.

He must have wanted to die very badly.

* * * * * * * * * * *

A fire station is a slice of life – and then some. We had ex-military, plumbers, carpenters, electricians, lawyers, notaries, welders, tin-bangers and roofers. We had saints and sinners.

We had all the pluses and all the minuses you'd find in any slice of society. We had rivalry, jealousy and bigotry.

We had a few guys who were practical jokers. One firefighter was having a few beers in the army mess and he got his hands on a thunder-flash. It was a big firecracker the army used to simulate a 36-hand grenade in training. One Sunday afternoon, as the guys were having a short nap, he asked the Captain if he could light the thunder-flash and put it under a garbage can. It would give the guys a good scare. The Captain said it was OK.

He went up to the bedroom, stuck the firecracker under the can and lit it. What an explosion! The can went into orbit and blew a ring in the ceiling. Two bedspreads caught fire and we thought we'd lost two guys. The officer on the watch desk was so scared he bit the end right off his pipe. We tidied things up and somebody took the bedspreads home and had them repaired. Nobody ever pulled a trick like that again.

Fun and Games

Every Frosh week at University, you can count on fire alarms being pulled on at least six floors. Good old freshmen – a bunch of drunken kids having lots of fun. Fun? Have your fun and enjoy life but don't jerk the Fire Department around.

Sometimes we'd get calls to the university at least four times a week, and the fun was wearing thin. When we answer a false alarm we do so with two pumpers, two aerials, a rescue vehicle and the Chief's car.

Why does the Chief arrive in his car? Why doesn't he arrive in the pumper or aerial with his men? It's because he has divisional responsibilities for several fire stations and might have to divide his duties with other fires elsewhere.

Pulling false alarms could leave a hole in fire protection if there was a major blaze somewhere else. It makes for longer response times and a chance of injury or loss of life.

But the kiddies at the U wanted their fun!

After about the fourth call the weather was turning cold. The temperature was 40° Fahrenheit and the Chief, Bob Butler, was really getting pissed off. He threatened to evacuate the residence if it happened again.

One of our smart-ass future leaders said to him: "You don't have that kind of power."

Bob blew. He lost it.

"Just fucking watch me!" He called for more equipment and more police and we began to evacuate the building.

The Dean was summoned. He told the Chief the kids were "only having fun". The dumb, left wing socialist fuck had a silver spoon stuck up his ass at birth and probably never had a real job in his entire life. He was somewhat pissed off about being called away from a cocktail party. Too fucking bad!

The good students in the building had to suffer along with the idiots.

Young, half-pissed female students in their nightgowns thought it was funny at first. They changed their minds when the nipples on their tits started to freeze and pucker up like gumdrops. They were starting to sober up. The male students were barfing and swearing. It finally dawned on the Dean that firefighters have a job to do and are not a bunch of dummies.

He yelled over a loud speaker that the next student who pulled a false alarm would be expelled for the rest of the semester. The false alarms stopped.

Code 9 – Lots Of Smoke

We were getting a lot of calls about a fire at a brand new shopping centre that hadn't yet opened.

There was lots of smoke.

A security guard was almost hysterical. He told us there was a teenage girl trapped inside. She'd been working in a store, preparing it for the Grand Opening. The building was secure. It was going to be tough breaking through steel and poured concrete.

"Where is she located?", the Captain yelled.

"Just behind that door."

Hold it! We inspected this place two weeks earlier and knew that the door had a push bar on it. All she had to do was push and the door would spring open.

"Not if there's a lock on it", says the guard.

I said: "City By-Laws say no locks on safety doors."

The guard replied: "The owner ordered us to lock it and put locks on all the doors."

Holy shit! The K-12 saw did its job. We cut off the hinges and the door fell open. We found a dead 17-year-old girl, black from smoke, with a look of terror on her face. Her fingernails were ripped out from scratching a locked metal door, and her eyes were full of pain, tears and fear.

Fuck!

Code 9 – Working Fire In The Business Section

We had a fire in a restaurant on a business block. As usual, there was a lot of smoke. The Captain, Keith Tucker, yelled to take out the big front window to help with ventilation. Wow! The glass had been in the window since the 1940s. We had to call for a sledge-hammer to do the job. Large shards of glass littered the sidewalk and street, but the pressure in the restaurant had been relieved.

It was 2.30 a.m. and we were tired and worn out. This was our ninth call since we started our shift at 6 p.m. the night before. I rubbed my eyes to clear them and I saw him. He was a man about 50 years of age and he was leaning against a telephone pole.

Instinctively, I knew! I yelled at the guy: "You bastard, you stupid bastard. You set this fire."

He yelled back at me: "How do you know? How the fuck do you know?"

The cops pulled up and I yelled for an officer to arrest the man. I told him that he'd set the fire. The cop put the puke in the cage in the back of the squad car, and I got my ass back in the restaurant to help pull down ceilings and open walls to check for fire extensions. Because of Captain Tucker's quick thinking in taking out the front window, we were able to get to the seed of the fire very quickly.

The arson squad and more cops arrived and asked to speak to me. The fire inspector told me the man admitted he was guilty but "is he ever pissed off with you."

"Who cares? He's a no-good puke."

They asked me how I knew he'd set the fire.

I told them I had taken a fire prevention course because if I was injured on a fire scene or in the line of duty I'd be able to transfer to the fire prevention unit. During the course, we learned a lot about fires – the way fire travels and the kind of people who set them. Along with pyromaniacs there are also pyronotics. They get a sexual rush from fires. When I saw the man at the telephone pole there was a full moon and it was very bright. I could see that he had a roaring hard on, so I put two and two together and made the call.

Medical Call in a High Rent Area
HOLY BEDPOST, BATMAN

We had a medical call in a high rent part of the city. It was a Code 10, which means wait for the police. We arrived first. What a shack.

It was 8 a.m. on a beautiful summer morning. The pump and ladder trucks pulled into the circular driveway. The dispatcher repeated again – Code 10 – wait for the police.

The Captain said to the dispatcher: "There's a lady screaming her head off. We're going in." We busted down the front door and went in.

We climbed a circular staircase and there she was – a 300-pound female tied to a bed. It was not a pretty sight. The Captain threw a blanket over her for modesty's sake. I took my knife out and cut the ropes on her arms and legs. She'd shit herself and pissed all over the bed. Her voice was hoarse from screaming.

The bed was a king size with a big headboard and strangely, there was a big dresser positioned at the foot. All of a sudden, we heard a moaning sound coming from the space between the bed and the wall.

A guy stood up, wearing the top half of a Batman suit. He was naked from the waist down and hung like a Tennessee mule.

"What's going on?" asks the Captain.

"I'm getting out of here", answered Batman.

He looked for something to cover his private parts and found his pants. We tried so hard not to grin but we all lost it.

I could hardly talk, I was laughing so hard. I said to the guy with an almost straight face: "What name should I put in my report?"

He replied: "Put down Batman. I'm outta here."

What happened? The well-to-do chubbette had called Rent-A-Dink or some such sex service place. She had a fantasy about being laid by Batman. He tied her up and stood on top of the dresser with his dick in his hand. He was supposed to jump and mount her.

He hit his head on the ceiling, bounced off her, hit his head against the wall and knocked himself cold. He'd been unconscious since 3 a.m.

The chubbette didn't care if he was dead or alive. She wanted out. So we came roaring to the rescue of the Caped Crusader and his Lady. We were sore from laughing.

* * * * * * * * * * * *

2.10 a.m. Medical Call

The call was supposed to be for a woman seven and a half months pregnant, who was going into early labour. When we arrived it was raining and very dark. The ambulance and two attendants had already arrived. I figured the dispatcher would recall us, but I decided to check just in case. I walked up to the attendants and asked: "Did you guys get the same call we did about a woman in labour?"

They said they did.

One of the attendants told us the husband was violent.

I told him: "Fuck, I can get pretty violent myself."

We walked up three flights of stairs and I could hear crying and screaming. I knocked on the door and a man's voice inside said: "Fuck off."

I said: "Open the door or you're going to hear two sounds."

He said: "What two sounds?"

I replied: "The sound of me kicking the door off its hinges and the sound of you cracking open your wallet to pay for a new door. You don't own this apartment. You rent it."

There was a pause before the door was opened a bit. I pushed it open the rest of the way. There was a woman on her back on the floor crying: "My water broke. My water broke."

I went to help her but the puke stood in front of me. I looked him straight in the eyes and told him to get the fuck out of the way or he'd hear two sounds.

"What two sounds?"

I told him: "The sound of me punching you right between your eyes and the sound of you hitting the floor. On second thought, you might not hear the second sound because you'll be out cold."

He got out of the way. I guess it was my John Gotti look that persuaded him. My wife says nobody hurts a woman when I'm around. Nobody!

I got down on the floor with her, took off her jeans and peeled down her panties. I had her legs wide open and her jeans were clinging to one ankle. One of the firefighters gave me a towel for under her behind.

"My water broke. My water broke", she kept screaming.

I said: "Don't worry. I've done this before. You're in good hands."

There was a tap on my shoulder.

Instinctively, I felt it was the puke and he was going to take a piece of me. I was ready to punch him in the nuts and put him out of commission. I was wrong. It was a police officer. He asked me to come with him. I told him: "I have a situation here."

He said: "She's not pregnant. She's a schizo and when she mixes alcohol with her schizo medication she thinks she's pregnant. Basically, her water didn't break. She pissed on you."

Yeah, so what else is new? Women have been pissing on me since I was nine years old. Everybody had a big laugh except the puke in the corner but fuck him.

"She's Going To Calf"

The dispatcher sent us out on a medical call. A woman in a car was in distress. The weather was great. Traffic was heavy and some people wouldn't even move over for the fire truck. Idiots!

We pulled up close to the car. I was on the radio trying to get more information from the dispatcher. Dennis, a big strong farm boy on my team, ran to the car to see what the problem was. He came running back to me, all excited, and yelled: "There's a lady in the car and she's gonna calf."

Bystanders started to laugh hysterically.

I asked: "Do you mean she's about to give birth?"

He answered: "Look, I'm off a farm and I know when someone is gonna calf."

I ordered two firefighters to drape a tarp over the side of the car for privacy. I tried to calm her down and reassured her I had done this before. I put on rubber gloves, removed her panties and spread her legs.

The baby was almost there. Then the paramedics stepped in and delivered a baby girl.

My face was the face and uniform she remembered and the new mother inserted a Birth announcement in the local paper thanking #12 fire crew. She called her baby girl Maitland, because that's the name of the street where she was born.

* * * * * * * * * * *

Another medical call came in at 4 a.m. A man was down. We were told to wait for Code 10. It might be a domestic disturbance.

When we arrived on the scene a lady in her nightgown met us. She was out on the lawn screaming: "My husband is bleeding and unconscious in the kitchen."

It didn't look like a domestic quarrel to me. It was just a scared woman concerned for her significant other. We went in to stabilize him before the ambulance arrived. The man was about 40. Wow! Was he ever out of it!

He was completely unconscious and there was blood, both from his head, and between the back of his legs.

What happened? His wife said a dripping sound coming from under the kitchen sink was keeping her awake. Her husband got under the sink, bare-naked, and was using a monkey wrench to tighten the plumbing.

His family jewels were dangling loose and swaying as he wrestled with the wrench. It was just at that moment the family cat, a big black sucker, saw something swinging and bit and scratched his nuts. He tried to scramble to his feet but he hit his head and knocked himself out trying to stand up under the sink.

We weren't supposed to laugh but we did. He recovered but he had a sore bag for a long time. I'd have shot that cat.

Code 9

Lots of smoke and flames were visible. Our information was that people were possibly trapped inside a two-storey brick house. It was really burning!

I yelled to one of my brother firefighters: "Haul your ass over here. It's you and me."

We dragged a hose through the smoke to the second floor. Before the introduction of air masks, we used to put hoses on part fog, and direct the fog in our faces, allowing us to breathe. We did that and still took a bad beating. I placed my hand on the door of one of the upstairs bedrooms and pulled it away pretty fast. It was red hot. We'd found the seed of the fire. We put the nozzle on full fog and kicked the door in. We walked across the room and took out a window with a fire axe. The room cleared of smoke quickly. Our Captain was real proud and very happy. We checked every room and did our circles. Thank God. No bodies!

We went back to the room where the fire started and I noticed something unusual. There were about 50 burned matches all over the floor. I told the Captain what I'd found. He asked the mother how many kids lived there.

She said: "Eight. Why?"

"Because my men found 50 matches on the floor in one bedroom. Whose room is it?"

She said it belonged to one of her sons, who was a "bit of a fire-bug". Then she said she was a "bit of a firebug, too" when she was a kid.

My Captain asked her: "What colour do you like?"

"Why?" she asked.

"Because we have blue, green, yellow and brown body bags, and I want to know what colour body bag to put you in when we come back."

She said: "You bastard. Get the fuck out of my house."

Back at the fire station the phone rang and someone on the other end ordered the Captain to go back to apologize. He was told, "You can't talk to the public like that."

I said to the Captain: "Let me handle this. I'm a bit more diplomatic than you are and if you grab her by the throat you'll be busted back to a first class firefighter."

He said: "OK, you smooth talking bastard. Go for it."

I pulled up to the fire scene and the lady was out on the lawn. I told her I was there representing the Captain and crew of #1 station and spoke for all. I told her I was apologizing.

She said: "Where's that fat fuck of a Captain?"

I told her he was up to his armpits in alligators. I tried to calm her down and told her I just wanted a couple of minutes of her time. She calmed down.

"I've only been a firefighter for a few years, but I've already dealt with at least 50 deaths. Most of them were fatalities from smoke inhalation, but others we could only identify from dental records."

I told her there's an expression about fire burn victims. It is "the living envy the dead". I told her she was a beautiful woman with beautiful children, and that we never wanted to come back to her house for a fire again.

I told her I'd seen lots of badly burned people and that my Captain had seen far more than me. "He's a good man and he cares."

She began to cry: "My God, I'm so sorry if I caused your men any problems. Can you get me some help for my son?"

I told her I could. I promised that an Inspector Robert Carruthers would come and talk with him that same afternoon.

"Will that help?"

She cried some more and hugged me. My heart went out to her. I had a couple of tears in my own eyes.

My Stove Pipes Fell Down

It was 4 a.m. and there was lots of smoke pouring out one door of a six-unit row house. A sweet little old lady was waiting on her veranda. It was dark and foggy outside. She told us her stovepipes fell down and that there was a lot of smoke inside.

I put a blanket around her. She wasn't really cold, just frightened. We entered the unit. It was a row house built in the 1920s, and when you get a fire in one of these old places you usually lose the whole row because there are no firewalls between them.

They were all individually heated with old space heaters, and stovepipes ran through walls to heat each of the rooms. The pipes got full of soot and gunk and had to be cleaned every so often.

The Captain said: "She's a sweet lady. Take all the pipes down and clean them in the backyard." The lady was so pleased, and said it was very kind of us. It was also good public relations for us.

Then the Chief came through the front door. He had a big cigar stuck in his jaw. His fire coat was wide open and his big gut was hanging out and over. He was a great sight at 4.30 a.m. He walked around the unit eyeballing everything.

By this time, the smoke had been cleared and the little old lady was back inside.

The Chief said to her: "Are you happy with the service?"

"Yes", she replied, "These fine men did a great job."

"Good!" he said. Before he left, he turned back to the little old lady and said: "Don't be ashamed lady, don't be ashamed. I used to live in a fucking dump like this one, too."

He had a way with words. He had a lot of class. I think he was a charm school dropout.

Pump One, Level One

Pump one, level one – which means take your time. It's a non-emergency. We were responding to a call from a neighbour in a posh area of the city.

I said to my Captain: "Man, this is a high rent area."

We arrived on the scene of a swish two-story home and there was no sign of a problem. A woman of about 50 walked through the snow, with a concerned look on her face. She said: "I'm sorry to call you out. I'm not a nosey neighbour but something's wrong. The couple who live in this house have been having some serious arguments lately and I think he left her. The mail and newspapers are in their mail box and the only footprints on the walk are from the paper boy this morning."

Our Captain sent Code 10 on his radio. We wanted police here because we were going to enter the house forcibly. We looked for the least expensive way to enter. Contrary to popular myths, we don't smash down doors with fire axes indiscriminately. We forced a basement window open and a junior man, three months on the job, went it. He came upstairs, opened the front door for us, and went back down to look around. Two big police officers in their 40s had appeared on the scene.

All of a sudden there was a scream – a horrifying scream, and the hairs came up on the back of my neck. It was our new man. He came rushing back upstairs, in shock, with a look of sheer terror on his face.

He couldn't say anything except "Downstairs, downstairs."

We went down the stairs to the basement, where the only source of light came from the basement windows. We found a pull chain and turned on an overhead bulb. There, hanging from the rafters, was a four-year old boy. He must have been hanging for four or five days and his neck was grotesquely stretched. The smell was so bad that even our tough old Captain started to retch.

We did a search of the house. We found the mother in bed with a smothered six-month-old baby. She had left a suicide note, which simply read: "I can't go on with life."

She had evacuated her bowels and the stench was over-powering. It made our eyes water. It was six of one, half dozen of another if my tears were from the smell or because of the trauma we had witnessed.

The coroner later said she had taken a lot of pills.

Bikers

In early 1965 I was transferred to a rough, tough area of town. It didn't bother me. It was like a homecoming. The signs of spring were all around – grass turning green, flowers, nice mini-skirts. If God made something better than pretty women, he has it hidden real well for Himself.

The Captain and I were in the kitchen of the fire station watching the goings on outside. Six big Harleys with bikers on board pulled into the lot of a restaurant across the street. One of the bikers' ladies dropped her leather pants, squatted, and took a leak. Real classy lady!

The Captain didn't have much time for bikers. I told him: "Captain, 99 percent of bikers are good people and wouldn't hurt a fly. They love their freedom. They stick together and have fun. They mind their own business and enjoy life. Some of them are mentally scarred from the Korean War or Vietnam. You can appreciate that."

He asked me if I was a biker.

I told him I loved bikes but I wasn't what you could call a biker. I told him I was a loner.

"No shit", he said. "You mix well with the men."

"Yes, I do. I love and respect them, but sometimes after a couple of deaths I jump on my Harley and just ride… destination unknown, back roads and little taverns. I flop in a small Ma and Pa motel or in my sleeping bag."

Across the street, the head biker left his girlfriend to watch over his Harley and crossed over to the fire station. He knocked on the front door.

The Captain left him to me, saying: "I don't want to talk to him. You handle him, Jimmy. From the looks of the bad bastards who come to visit you at this station, I know you can handle him."

"OK! You're the Boss!"

I opened the station door and said: "How can I help you, Sir?"

He smiled a crooked smile. A few teeth were missing. There was a scar on his left cheek that extended all the way down to his chin. He hadn't shaved or showered for a week. He was also wearing a sanitary napkin around his neck as a talisman. Some fashion statement! But it's his life – not mine. He's free. He can dress anyway he chooses.

He asked: "Who's in charge of this station?"

I told him I was in charge at the moment, and asked again if I could help him.

He lightened up a little. I invited him in and asked him to sit in the kitchen and have a coffee with me. "From the kitchen you can keep an eye on your Harley."

He smiled and asked: "You like bikes?"

I told him I loved bikes and that I had a 1958 Harley. I told him I'd been riding since I was 14 years old.

He said: "I've never seen you around."

I told him, just as I had told the Captain, that I was a loner and kept to myself.

He replied "We all march to the tune of a different drummer. I'm a Vietnam veteran and I'm just doing my thing."

I answered him: "Good attitude… live and let live."

He said: "We like you guys on the fire department. You do nothing but good. The pigs – the cops – they're another story. They cause us lots of grief. They're always stopping us for chicken shit like not having a front brake on our choppers. Shit, man, if you hit something, what difference does it make if you have one brake or two? You're just as dead!"

I was starting to like this guy. I had flashbacks to my boyhood and my old neighbourhood. My father was a big, rough Irish construction foreman who installed fire hydrants. He was so strong he could pick a hydrant up.

The biker, whose name was "Chopper", began to talk. "IF (he emphasized the 'if') IF."

"If what?"

He said: "If our clubhouse burns down, DON'T go in. There's a biker war going on and there might be dynamite in the basement. So, DON'T go in. If the pigs want to go in, that's OK. We don't like pigs anyway. I'm not saying it's going to burn but with a biker war going on you never know."

He stood up, sauntered across the floor to the sink and rinsed out his coffee mug.

I said to him: "Thanks for the information and the respect."

He said: "Fuck, man, us bikers gotta stick together."

He smiled and walked down the long hallway to the front door. I bade him farewell and said "Good luck, good riding."

He turned and said "Same to you" and smiled again. "I gotta get back to my crew."

The Captain came into the kitchen. The sound of a Harley firing up is noise to some but it's music to my ears. The Captain said, "Is there anybody you don't know?"

Two weeks later the bikers' clubhouse burned and there were no injuries. We fought the fire from the outside. When a biker talks, listen and heed!

Still on bikers, a chopper was racing down the Queensway – doing "wheelies" and showing off. He lost it because he was going too fast when he tried to get off at an exit. My crew and I pulled up. He was a mess.

One of my men, Art MacNamara, was a great guy to have on our team, because he'd been in the ambulance service before joining the fire department.

Art said to me: "Captain, this young man is quite drunk and he's lost his left thumb. Before he loses consciousness, will you be my witness?"

"Sure, what do you want to do, Art?"

"Come with me, Captain."

We approached the young biker and Art asked him: "Can you understand me, sir?"

He mumbled a "yes".

The crew had placed him on a stabilizer board and he was ready to be transferred to hospital.

Art asked him if he wanted a thumb or a big toe.

"What do you mean?" he mumbled.

Art told him: "Your hand is bandaged and you've lost your left thumb down to the bone. The Captain is my witness and if you say "yes" when you get to hospital, your left toe will be amputated and it'll replace your left thumb. Do you understand?"

"Yes, I do!"

"You heard that, Captain?"

"Yes, I did, Art."

When the ambulance arrived I sent Art along to explain the situation at the hospital. Art was well known at the hospital from his days in the ambulance service. It was a great call for Art to make.

The young biker lost his license for a year and his left big toe.

When he was released from hospital, he came to the fire station to thank us and to show off his new thumb-toe. I told him to thank Art because it was his call.

"My New Car Is A Write-off?"

It was a lovely Sunday morning in the summer. We had a couple of shit calls but nothing serious. The loudspeaker blared out that there had been a motor vehicle accident also involving a train. The railway crossing was not far from the fire station and we were there in a matter of minutes.

We saw it as soon as we turned the corner. It was a huge diesel electric train. The train had the right of way and two women had driven around the warning barriers. The train pushed the car a half a mile down the tracks.

We walked the rocky bed beside the tracks. We knew that no one could survive an accident like that. The two ladies smelled of alcohol and were very, very dead. Every bone in their bodies was broken. So sad, so stupid. Another useless, alcohol related death scene.

The car didn't catch fire, which was unusual given the impact and the sparks from the train. We forced the car door open and obtained driver and car information from the glove compartment. Later, after the bodies were removed, we gave the information to the Chief and went back to cleaning fire trucks. The Chief came out of his office with a real stunned look on his face.

He said: "I've been on this job for 34 years and I have never had a conversation like that."

I said: "What do you mean?"

"Usually the police contact relatives in the event of a fatal accident but they were busy and asked me to make the call. I asked for the husband and told him his wife had been involved in a fatal accident. Do you know what he asked? He asked me: 'How's my car?'

I told him it was a write-off and he said: 'My new car is a write-off?'

Yes, I said.

Then he said: 'I'm glad the cunt's dead' and hung up on me. That must have been one happy home."

Here, Pussy

Peter and I came back from a fire call – a chicken shit call for a cat up a tree. We put a ladder up, put on some fire mitts and went up. After we left, the stupid cat ran right back up the tree. The woman phoned the Chief's office to get us to go back. The Chief said NO. He told the lady his men could get hurt rescuing the cat and, besides, the cat would come down by itself when it got hungry.

The lady became verbally abusive. The Chief stopped her in her tracks when he said "Look lady, when's the last time you saw the skeleton of a cat in a tree?" That ended the conversation.

Hookers Who Have Known Me

It was embarrassing to walk through the lower town Market with my wife and children. All the hookers knew me because my fire station was in the centre of their world. We got the odd call to minister to one of them when one fell off a curb or tripped over her six-inch fuck-me high heels after one too many.

When our crew went out on a medical assist call, I had the job of putting an elastic bandage on a well-turned ankle, or I'd have to calm the victim down until an ambulance and police arrived.

Occasionally, some bastard pimp would beat them up. Sick, evil bastards. The hookers got to know and like me and they'd tickle my son and make him laugh.

One beautiful day we were sitting on a bench outside the fire hall around 2:00 p.m. We were enjoying a quiet time between fire calls. Our neighbours were out on their verandas and balconies doing the same thing. All of a sudden, a big 1964 Chrysler convertible with four hookers in it drove by.

The car stopped half a block away. The driver spun her wheels in reverse, stopped in front of us, and yelled: "There's Jimmy. He fixed my leg." One of the other hookers was half drunk and she screamed: "Someday we'll come into the fire hall and gang bang all you fucking guys."

The Chief was not amused. He came out of the station and ordered us all inside. I thought it was funny. The neighbours didn't. We had lots of complaints, but screw them if they can't take a joke.

I enjoyed my service at the hookers' station and have many happy memories.

Some of the nicest ladies I've ever met in my life were hookers and exotic dancers. It's so easy to take other people's inventories. Who knows why some people branch off in different directions? The only person who ever walked the earth who was perfect had nail holes in his feet and hands, and that wasn't you or me!

Captain, My Captain

Every job in this wonderful world has its winners and losers. Our Captain had another Captain fill in for him one weekend while he and his wife attended an out of town wedding. The substitute Captain was a stickler for the rules, and not in the same league as our regular.

This guy was right by the book; you're here to fight fires and work, not to have any fun, so the workplace wasn't very pleasant. We showed respect, obeyed orders and did as we were told. It was only for a weekend after all.

After every call our substitute Captain had nothing but negative things to say about our firefighting ability. He knew everything and he wanted everyone to know it.

We got a call from a construction site about 2:30 a.m. Sunday morning. It was nothing serious – just some rubbish smouldering in a garbage pail in a construction shack. We broke down the door (that's what firefighters do) and threw the pail out into the snow.

There were still some papers smoking on the floor in the corner where the pail had been. The Captain said to Warner Bradley: "Take that bucket of water over there and throw it on the papers in the corner."

Warner said: "I don't think it's water, Captain."

The Captain barked at him: "You'll do as you're told or I'll have you charged."

Warner said: "OK. You're the boss."

He threw the contents of the pail on the hot papers. The pail was full of naphtha fuel. The construction shack burned to the ground while one big, stupid, stubborn know-it-all Captain was screaming: "No one tell anyone about this."

"Yes, Captain, it'll be our secret."

The whole department knew about it overnight. We had sore ribs for days from laughing. That Captain never subbed for ours again.

* * * * * * * * * * *

Sometimes we do get our comeuppance from an M.D. We responded to a fire at a lab in a hospital and a doctor told us not to go in. He said it was too dangerous.

The Captain said: "Don't tell me what to do! I'm a firefighting Captain and I have more powers than the police."

The doctor said: "OK, but there are little vials in there and they hold Yellow Fever, Cholera, Diphtheria, Anthrax and AIDS viruses. They can be lethal if they're airborne. But, go ahead, go on in."

Needless to say, the Captain had a change of heart!

"I'm Only 55, You Son Of A Bitch"

The dispatcher sent us out on a medical call. He said we'd only need the pump. We were being called to a possible cardiac arrest, and the ambulance had been delayed, so we were on our own.

We were relatively new to the healing arts. Every firefighter is taught basic first aid in five areas – bleeding, breathing, shock, stabilization and comfort. Hey, what else is there?

Some firefighters have no difficulty with medical calls, but others, depending on the nature of the call, such as suicide with a shotgun, someone chopping off his penis or drinking Drano, will have their emotions scrambled for quite awhile. Today, after a bad injury or suicide, counsellors come in and talk to the firefighters. In the 60s we just went out and got drunk. Trauma shown on TV is not the same as in real life. On TV they don't shit, piss, bleed and puke on you. We were into real life – not TV dramatization.

Our medical call was at an Italian house party. The Captain and I went in. There was lots of singing and dancing, and the vino was flowing freely. A woman told us in broken English that the problem was in the basement rec room. A man was on the floor clasping his chest.

At first, it looked like an attempted homicide. It appeared that someone had hit him on the head with a meat cleaver. It turned out that his cheap hairpiece had come loose and the only thing keeping it on his head were two sticky tabs. His red face made it look like a mob hit – meat cleaver style.

The dispatcher asked the Captain: "What do you have?"

The Captain answered: "We have a 60-year-old male down."

At that, the man glared at the Captain with an if-looks-could-kill look: "I'm 55, you son of a bitch, I'm 55."

Good old male vanity.

"Flames Came Out Of My Ass"

I like them, I love them, I respect them, but in this whole wide world there is no more mentally fucked up group of people than firefighters. Maybe it's the things we see and have to deal with. Who knows?

As I said, God didn't make me a rocket scientist. He made me something much more important... a man, a husband, a father, a friend and right up there with all those attributes he made me a fire-fighter. God, I didn't just like my job. I loved it.

A firefighter has to remember there is lots of idle time in a fire station, and the devil finds work for idle hands. There are two phone systems in an average station – a system at the watch desk for incoming 911 calls and a handset on the wall for personal calls. As much as I love and respect my brother firefighters, I never trusted them. If you didn't want your life story to travel over the speed of sound – shut your mouth. You never knew who would pick up an extension on the personal phone.

Lorne had big time asshole trouble and had to be hospitalized for surgery. Forty years ago, it was major surgery and meant a few days on your back in hospital.

Lorne tried to keep his secret but after a few beers it slipped out. When his time came, we were working a 24-hour shift on a Sunday and one of the guys phoned him in the hospital and asked him if he wanted some real food instead of "that hospital shit."

"Yeah", he said.

Sunday is traditionally spaghetti and meatball lunch in a fire station. Some of the best basic cooks are firefighters. We had an Italian guy named Luigi who made the best spaghetti and meatballs in the world.

We called our Chief and asked him if he would deliver dinner to Lorne in the hospital. He said "sure" and took some of Little Italy's finest cooking with him. Early the next morning, the phone rang. It was Lorne.

He was yelling and screaming: "I'll get even with every one of you fucking guys. My arsehole is on fire and I have tears as big as horse balls rolling down my face. I went to take a dump and flames came out of my ass. You pack of fucks. Which one of you bastards doctored the meatballs? I only had my operation on Friday. The meatballs blew the cotton packing right out of my ass."

Lorne did manage to pay us back...

Two weeks later, he was back on the job. There were a few snickers here and there and some restrained smiles and laughter.

Lorne said: "It's nice to be back to work with my best buddies, and thanks for the spaghetti and meatballs." Everybody broke up.

"Boy, you pack of assholes got me real good. I'll tell you, it sure cauterized the old ring." More laughter.

In the 1960s we bought milk in glass quart bottles – not the plastic shit we have today. Lorne said: "Hey, you guys, my brother's a milkman. He was by the house this morning and gave us a treat. He gave me six quarts of chocolate milk – free – right off the milk wagon. Fill your boots, guys."

Hey, something free in a fire station. Go for it. With eight guys on duty, six quarts didn't last very long. It was a cold morning, 20° below zero F. The gong hit – single dwelling – no exposures – vacant house waiting for demolition. It was an outside fire and lines were laid. Eight guys to fight a fire and the only one smiling was Lornie. Lorne's creed was "don't get mad, get even". He'd bought six quarts of chocolate milk and six packages of Ex-Lax. There were seven guys frozen cock stiff with shitty pants.

"Don't tell anyone I shit my pants."

"Don't worry" Lorne said "I'll take your secret to my grave."

Back at the station Lorne was on the watch desk and seven fire-fighters were in the showers. All you could smell were armpits and assholes. Lorne phoned the dispatcher to put in an all-station call: "Anyone who wants to buy chocolate milk laced with Ex-Lax, call Lorne at #1 station."

Don't get mad. Get even!

Never A Dull Moment

Fire fighting and fire calls are never the same. You never know exactly what you have on your hands until you arrive and survey the scene. But there's never a dull moment.

Our dispatcher told us we had a medical call. There was a male in a snow bank. It was a possible 10-12 – a drunk.

It was 3:00 a.m. and cold – about -30°F. It was our fifth call since we started our shift. We were tired but, as always, we were ready to rock and roll.

The dispatcher told us the ambulance would be delayed. This call was going to be very different and very, very strange. The guy in the snow bank was going to turn out to be a prizewinner.

Our Captain radioed the dispatcher for more information. The only information he had was that an unknown male was in a snow bank on the front lawn of a high-rise ghetto type building. We wandered around until we found the nutbar.

Holy shit, this guy was dead. Call the police. The Captain told the dispatcher we had a Code 5 – a death – and that we needed a coroner.

"Hey, Captain, this guy doesn't have any thumbs."

The Captain sent me to take a look. The guy was frozen solid and he really didn't have any thumbs. The police arrived. One of the detectives examined the corpse.

"Shit, I know him. He's a drug dealer and a pimp. We've had calls to his apartment – #904 – many times. He's a loser – no great loss."

After the ambulance and coroner arrived we followed the detectives into the building and took an elevator to the ninth floor and unit #904. The door was unlocked, and there was blood all over the place. There was a big set of bolt cutters on the floor, and nearby, a pair of thumbs.

The detectives figured that some goons paid him a visit, intending to throw him off the balcony. They cut off his thumbs when he tried to save himself – look Ma, no thumbs. They must have had a running start when they pitched him over the railing. Good fucking bye. He was airborne. He fell 37 feet away from the building.

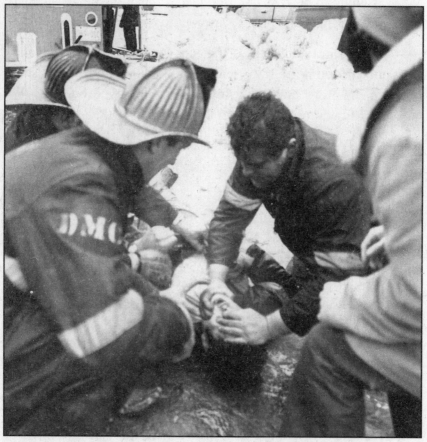

A 14,000-volt hydro line fell on a pumper. Jimmy Walsh unknowingly came in contact with the truck. He was thrown 20-feet and was clinically dead. His teeth were clenched shut and I couldn't give him "mouth to mouth." I gave him mouth to nose. It may have been the very first time a man was brought back from the dead this way. Jimmy lived.

Steve Brabazon (pictured at left) and six others of my Ottawa fire-fighting brothers were volunteers in "the hole" at the carnage of the New York World Trade Towers.

(Below) Steve's fingers point to the remnants of a New York firefighter's coat, which was identified and presented to the widow, giving her some small comfort and closure.

(Above) Some firefighters still believe beer and booze will wash away the horror of a "bad one" – especially when children die. After joining AA, I exorcised my demons by riding my Harley-Davidson motorcycle alone over back roads, spending the night in a sleeping bag or in a Ma and Pa motel.

(Left) My beautiful wife Sharon (a talented Canadian artist) and I. We've been together for over forty years. Visit Sharon's website at: www.creativecrafts.ca

I'm A Doctor

We were called out to a car accident. A man was coming back from an Italian wine festival and ran into a tree. He should have died but didn't.

His feet went up and under the dash. His head went through the window and came back in. His throat was cut but he was lucky, he hadn't severed an artery. We were doing the best we could.

There was a knot of people standing around so I asked if anybody had medical experience. One guy said he was a doctor. What luck!

I said: "Am I ever glad to see you. Can you give me a hand?"

He walked over to the car, grabbed the guy by the shoulder and tried to yank him out.

I said: "For God sakes Almighty, you're going to kill him. What kind of a doctor are you?"

He replied that he worked in a veterinary hospital just down the street.

I told him to fuck off. Shortly afterwards, the Chief came by. He was very impressed with the first aid job we had done. It was nice to get a pat on the back instead of the usual kick in the arse.

Strange and Wonderful People

Firehouses, fire halls, fire stations. Ever since the first one was built they've been central venues in the community. We have some wild and crazy people wandering in and out at all hours of the day and night. I could write volumes just about the characters.

One fellow who dropped in regularly was a very old, shell-shocked veteran from World War 1. He served his country, but his country didn't reward the sacrifice. He was poor and subsisted on a very small disability pension. They call it the "burned out pension".

He was harmless. He'd been married for 54 years and when his wife died and his children moved away we became his only family.

When I first met him, he always seemed to be adjusting his teeth. I asked our Captain one night: "Sir, would it offend the old veteran if I slipped him a few dollars to buy some of that paste that old people use to keep their teeth in?"

The Captain said: "Have you ever noticed that just about every day he's wearing a different set of teeth?"

"Not really, Captain. I never looked that closely."

The Captain said: "One day he'll have a gold tooth or a couple of silver teeth and some days he'll have a combination of both."

"How the hell does he get a mix of teeth like that?"

The Captain said: "The funeral parlour is just around the corner. When people die they aren't buried with their teeth. The plates are recycled and sent to Third World countries. So he goes in the back, looks through the drawer where they're kept, and if they fit, he wears them."

Not a terribly uplifting conversation just before lunch.

The poor old guy passed away in 1991 when he was 97. God rest his soul. I wonder if St. Peter has drawers full of spare dental plates.

A Way With Words

It was a quiet, relaxing sunny afternoon. The Captain and a brand new rookie were sitting on a bench in front of the station. The rookie was a bit of a big mouth and a know-it-all for someone only nine months on the job. They were shooting the breeze, exchanging small talk.

The Captain had more mud on his boots than that rookie would ever see. He was a 50-year old World War 11 vet who'd been to Hell and back.

On the other side of the street they saw a smashing lady headed their way. She was nicely dressed and looked like a million bucks.

The smart-ass rookie said to the Captain: "Hey, Sir, do you bang them when they're that old?"

The Captain was taken aback. He said: "Pardon me?"

The rookie asked: "Would you screw that?"

The Captain said: "Just a second, I'll ask her. Hey, lady, this rookie wants to know if you screw at your age?"

I thought the rookie was going to choke. The lady was the Captain's wife. You win some and you lose some, but you lose more often when you have a big mouth.

It was a listen and learn day for the rookie. Had it been the wrong Captain or the wrong firefighter he might have ended up with the shit kicked out of him.

A Blue Veiner

One of the Lieutenants in our station lost his wife. He was a man who was born to be married, and after a respectable period of mourning, he began looking for another woman to share his life. Like me, he enjoyed being married and wanted to have a lady in his life.

My wife, Sharon, told her girl friend that if she died, I would get married again. She said: "Jimmy is just like all men. He loves having a woman in his life and besides that, he likes to get laid."

The Lieutenant met another good woman and they went away for a dirty weekend to get to know each other better. When he undressed she looked him up and down. He was hung like a horse. She said: "What's that?" He wasn't circumcised and she told him: "I like you, but I'd appreciate it if you'd get circumcised."

He replied: "I'm 42 years old but if it'll make you happy I'll have it done."

So he went to a hospital and got himself clipped. The guys at the fire station found out and had a copy of Playboy Magazine sent to him "Special Delivery". You can probably guess the rest. He started to read the magazine (who doesn't read Playboy?). He had a blue veiner and popped four stitches. He wasn't a happy officer. Like most firefighters, he didn't get mad, he got even. But that's another story.

Never A Dull Moment

Fire stations are 24-hour operations. We never close. People who visit them are like casts of characters from a Grade B movie. My God, there's never a dull moment. There is also a very special relationship between firemen and policemen. I guess we have a special respect for one another because we deal a lot with the same people, places and things. My brother, Johnny, was a police officer. He came into the firestation one evening about 11.30 p.m. He was almost pissing his pants, laughing so hard he could hardly stand up. I asked him: "What's so funny?"

He said he was manning a speed trap and stopped a speeding car with two teenagers in it. They were both about 17. The young male was polite but he was in a hurry to be off.

"He said to me: 'Can you speed it up, please?'

I looked at him. I told him I was young too a long time ago, and if he could give me a good reason why he was speeding, I'd let him off with a warning – no speeding ticket.

He looked first at his girl friend and then at me. He said: 'We were screwing and the condom broke and I have to get her home fast to douche'.

That's good enough for me, I said, GO!"

What Goes Around Comes Around

One of our crew, Ray Callaghan, later to become a Chief in Florida, didn't feel like doing drill, so he asked the Captain if he could videotape everybody doing ladder drill – sort of a training film.

The Captain put us through a real Cecil B. DeMille production laying hoses and everything else, while Ray ran around, busily filming. As time passed, the Captain kept asking Ray when he was going to bring the tape in and play it for him.

Ray didn't even have a tape in the video camera. A real nutbar. He was just too hung-over to drill.

Another character at #11 station thought he'd be funny. He was painting the tower and threw a dummy off, to make us think someone had fallen.

He didn't realize there was a little old lady sitting in the backyard. She had a heart attack.

He was in very deep shit over that stupid caper.

Suicide

A medical call came in. We responded with one pump truck. It was a call to a rough part of town, not far from the station. There was a woman on the lawn with a young baby in her arms.

The ambulance was delayed, and we thought we had a Code 5 – a death or suicide – on our hands, so the police were called in. I informed the dispatcher.

The young woman with the baby screamed: "In there... in there."

She looked about 14 – a baby with a baby. We went into a unit of row housing and down the stairs to the basement.

I said: "Somebody shit themselves."

Then I said to the dispatcher: "Send Code 10 NOW."

"They're delayed, Captain."

"Tell them I don't give a shit. I need Code 10 (Police response) NOW."

We had found the problem in the dimly lit basement. A young man, maybe 20 years old, was hanging from a rafter. He had kicked a box out from underneath himself. My heart started to pound. In the subdued lighting, I could barely make out his shoulder length, auburn hair. For a split second I thought it could be my oldest son, who was red haired, hanging there!

"Cut him down! NOW!"

"Yes, Sir."

We knew in our heart of hearts that he was stone dead, but we never leave anything to chance. He was beyond any help. Sometimes we can bring people back from the brink of death, but not this guy. Finally the police, ambulance and coroner arrived.

We returned to the station, backed the pump in the big door, parked it and washed all our lifesaving first-aid equipment.

It was time for a shift change. I was turning over the watch to the in-coming Captain. The phone rang. It was for me, the Captain in charge of the last call.

I said: "Come on, guys, we're going back to that hanging."

We fired up the pump and drove the short distance back to the suicide. Two detectives were standing on the grass. One guy had a toothpick stuck in a mouth you'd like to punch in. I walked across the lawn.

"I know why you called us back", I said to the detectives.

"What are you, psychic or something?" said the smart ass with the toothpick. "Why did you cut him down?"

That's when I lost it.

"You asshole. That wasn't an anti-police thing. My three brothers are police officers in this city. It's your fucking attitude with that Dick Tracy toothpick in your smart-ass mouth. Don't you have brains enough to figure out what we have here? We have a drug dealer who just did himself. We have a young mother with a baby she's going to have to provide for. As young as she is, she knows the system and how it works. Can you imagine a court case where she sues the fire department and me? Can you imagine her lawyer asking her what the fire department did when they saw her boyfriend hanging there? Can you just imagine her answer? 'Nothing, because they said it was a police matter'. My men and I would never own anything again. We'd be sued for everything we had. Understand?"

"Yes, Sir."

"See ya!"

Game, set and match. I was very proud of myself. I'd had great men train me to think, not to just go by a book – Thank God.

"Got a Light?"

We responded to a fire call in Lowertown. The lady told the Chief her dog started the fire. She said he was playing with matches. The Chief turned to her and said: "I'm so glad to meet you. I have a cat that smokes and he doesn't know how to light his cigarettes. I'd like to borrow your dog so he can light my cat's smokes."

My Baby's Inside

It was May and raining. What would today bring?

The answer came soon enough. We had a working fire and possibly people trapped inside. We rolled out with the pump, aerial trucks, a rescue vehicle and emergency car. An ambulance was on the way and police had been called in on Code 10.

When we arrived there was plenty of smoke, and flames were licking out a second storey window. We laid our lines and hooked on to the pump.

Bob Tremblay was with me on the back of the pump. He was great to work with, even though he was a neat and clean freak.

A woman on the lawn was screaming her head off: "My baby's inside, my baby's inside."

Bob went in the front door and started his circle. It was hot and smokey. Another shit kicking.

I went to the screaming woman and asked her what room her baby was in. She pointed to the window where smoke and flames were belching. Bob had ventilated the house by smashing windows.

I found Bob in the room fighting with the "baby".

Baby? Her baby was a six foot seven inch, 290-pound linebacker. He was built like a brick shithouse and his arms were the size of tree trunks. He'd been smoking dope in bed and set it on fire.

He was big, tough, stoned and scared. He took a swing at Bob. Burned skin on his arm came off and wrapped around Bob's neck like a boa constrictor. Was he impressed!

We fought with him and dragged him downstairs. He had third degree burns on his shoulder and right arm and second degree burns on his chest and frontal area. His face was unmarked.

The gorilla wanted to tangle assholes with us. Now we were really having a hard time holding him down, but it wasn't his day. He was too stoned. His Mom was giving him shit as we loaded him into the ambulance.

"Smarten up, you stupid bastard, and listen to the nice fire-fighters."

Some baby!

It's back to the station and we hit the showers. If you don't want to get dirty – sell shoes.

Captain Bob and Mark

Captain Bob was good people. He was decent and fair, but stern. He had a 14-year old son, Mark, who went to school in my area.

Mark was an accident that wasn't supposed to happen. Captain Bob had a vasectomy years earlier. When his wife got pregnant he became very suspicious and went back to his doctor.

The doctor examined him and Bob was told he had a third vas cord – unusual but not all that rare.

Bob and his wife had been looking forward to travelling and other luxuries. His two older kids were in university, when all of a sudden – WHAM – a new baby, diapers, and all that jazz.

They accepted their life-changing experience and Bob used to kid: "Hey, I get to talk to all the young mommies at Mark's hockey games."

Mark came home later than usual one night. His curfew was 11:00 p.m. and it was closer to 1:00 a.m. when he rolled in. He reeked of alcohol.

Captain Bob and his wife talked. Bob said: "Look, our two older children are at college, and we have to concentrate on Mark. My mother left me a few thousand dollars. I thought we'd use it to travel but this is more important. I think we should enroll Mark in a private school. It's expensive but it might pay for itself in the long run."

So Mark was shipped off to a private boarding school. It was a whole new ballgame for him – lots of discipline, uniforms and "Yes, Sir" and "No, Sir".

One day in the classroom the teacher said: "Let's talk about our families and what they do."

One kid said his father owned an oil company in Saudi Arabia.

"He's very important and I love him, but I only see him on holidays and in the summer. He's worth seven billion dollars."

Donald Sutherland's son, Keifer, was one of the students, and there were others whose mothers were well known actresses and often away on movie sets.

One kid said: "My father's dead but my mother's a famous movie actress. She travels all over the world and I won't see her again for three months. She's making a movie in India." And so the stories of the rich and famous unfolded.

Then the teacher asked: "What does your Dad do, Mark?"

"He's a firefighting Captain, Sir!"

Almost in unison the whole class said, "WOW! Can we meet him?" The teacher said: "I second that. When can we meet him?"

The phone rang at the station and it was Mark for his father.

"Hi Dad, it's Mark. I'm phoning from school."

"Yeah, what kind of shit are you in now?"

"None Dad. Can you come to the school with a fire truck? All the kids want to meet you and your crew."

Bob was delighted Mark wasn't in the doo doo. He phoned the Chief's office and advised him we were going to inspect a private school that afternoon. At 1:30 p.m., Captain Bob arrived at the school with a pump, an aerial, and a rescue vehicle.

Everyone in the school, including the teachers, wanted to meet Captain Bob and his firefighters. All the super-rich kids with important parents were green with envy, not just because he was a firefighter, but because Mark had his father there to love and hug him.

The kids had the time of their lives jumping into the fire net and crawling over the fire trucks, and to boot, they got to meet some very real, non-plastic people – firefighters.

It had to be the best day of the Captain's life. Somehow, it made everything worthwhile.

It's Not All Work

A couple of our young bucks went out on the town together. One of them was a smoothie and both of them were ladies' men.

They were in a downtown bar looking over a gorgeous blond who had just slinked in. One bet his buddy he could get lucky with her.

"Watch me!"

He walked over to the Madonna and said: "Were you hurt when you fell down from Heaven?" She had a sense of humour and they got along famously.

Then he tried another line on her, asking if she was a model. She liked that. She said she was a legal secretary and asked what he did for a living.

He didn't want to tell her he was a firefighter so he told her he was a fashion photographer. He said he was on assignment for Playboy magazine. He told her it was a great job with lots of travelling.

Then he said: "Let's not talk about me. Let's talk about you. How do you like working for a lawyer?"

She said it was OK but she was bored.

Then she started asking him about Playboy. How much were models paid? He told her if one made it big time, she could earn as much as $100,000 for Playgirl of the Year, plus maybe a chance at the movies.

She didn't want to talk about anything else. She said: "What about me? Would I be a good model?"

He said he really couldn't tell because she had clothes on. Then he said he had lost his business cards and his company credit cards.

She said: "That's OK. I have credit cards. What do you need?"

He said he had to book into a first class hotel. She said OK.

Then he said he needed a camera. No sooner said than done. He took pictures of her clothed and unclothed, and told her it wasn't going to work. He said: "No offence, but you're just too white. You need some tanning."

He told her he was coming back in a month's time and he'd take her to Jamaica or Nassau to put a tan on her.

She said: "No, let's go now. I have credit cards." So they flew off to Jamaica. He told her to save every receipt and Playboy would reimburse her. He said to send her expense account to Hugh Heffner at the Playboy mansion in Chicago.

He phoned the Chief's office and booked time off sick. They had a wonderful time in Jamaica.

They returned home and went their separate ways. She contacted Playboy and was told no such person worked for them. Her expense account was returned to her.

Months later, there was a fire call to her office building. Our super stud stepped off the side of the fire truck and right into her path.

Her civil action was settled 50-50. The judge had a great laugh.

Flying Fish

We had one fanatic who lived to fish. Every day he was off – summer or winter – he fished.

One day he was in the backyard of our station with his new rod, practicing casting. He threw the line out and it got snagged on an overhead utility line.

Somebody phoned the dispatcher, who put out an all-stations call – anybody who wants to learn how to catch flying fish get in touch with Al at the station.

Al was some pissed off!

Let's Kill All The Lawyers

Darren came on the fire department for all the wrong reasons. He had a bad attitude. He'd been to Law School for two years, just long enough to think he was smarter than he was, and knew much more than we did. He looked down on us as the great unwashed.

He may have been right but his attitude sucked big time. He really needed an attitude transplant. Most of the men on the department were guys with a background in the military or they were miners, plumbers, carpenters and electricians. Some of them were minor pro hockey and football players, but they were men who got their hands dirty and knew the meaning of hard work. Darren figured that because he had two years of Law School under his belt that his shit didn't stink. The fact is that most of the Second World War veterans I had for officers had PhDs in real life, and knew things you don't learn in classes or from books.

One night, Darren was doing the radio test. All he had to do was say "#7 pump to dispatcher. You're coming in loud and clear."

George Maxwell said to me: "I'm going to straighten that asshole Darren out. Play along with me. Tell Darren he's wanted on the phone. I'll be on the upstairs extension."

I said over the speaker: "Darren, wall phone." George had clued us in as to what he was going to say. On the upstairs extension, he said in mellow tones: "Hi, I'm Fred Crawford from NBC News in New York City. I'm here visiting and I was on a tour of the Communications Centre when I heard this golden voice coming over the speaker. I asked whose voice it was and an Inspector told me: 'That's Darren. He's a junior fireman at #7 fire hall.' I said: 'That man has a voice made for radio and TV. How can I get to talk to him?' I got #7 fire hall's phone number and that's why I'm calling. Have you ever thought of a career in broadcasting?"

By this time, Darren was wetting his shorts. He got off the phone and he was white. I asked him what the hell was wrong. I told him he looked like he'd seen a ghost. He told us what the man from NBC had said. Darren confessed that he'd love a job in TV or radio.

George came downstairs and casually asked: "What's going on?"

Darren told him that the man from NBC was going to call him again the first of the next week on the day shift.

George told him: "You'd better start to practice, practice..."

"What?" asked Darren.

"Practice reading the news. I'll help you", said George, "Get a chair and a newspaper."

George took Darren out on the apparatus floor and told him: "Put your chair at the end of the hard suction on the side of the pump and practice reading the news."

The dumb bastard stood on a chair and said: "And now for the latest news."

George would say: "Not bad, do it again, lower your voice and have more feeling."

We were pissing ourselves laughing. I don't know how George managed to keep a straight face. Every day for a week, George went upstairs, I'd pick up the phone and Darren would have his talks with the fictitious man from NBC.

The next week, Darren phoned NBC in New York. They thought he was a froot loop and asked him where he worked. When he told them he worked at a fire station they asked him: "Do you think there's a possibility that you've been had by your mates?"

Darren put two and two together and got five and he was some pissed off. He asked for a transfer and got one. Then he quit and went back to Law School.

Shakespeare was right when he said: "Kill all the lawyers!"

Give Us This Day..

I was Acting Captain when the call came in. A train at a level crossing had hit a woman's car. We were first on the scene. I guessed she was about 72 years old, and she was badly busted up. Every bone in her body was broken, and she was badly mangled. She was what we call VSA – Vital Signs Absent.

There was little point waiting for the Para-medics or the Coroner. She was folded up like a string of cooked spaghetti. It was devastating to view such mutilation on a human body. We removed her from the vehicle and placed her on a tarpaulin. I gently wrapped her up and laid her back on the ground. I wanted to say a prayer for her in this private moment, so I knelt, bowed my head, and clasped my hands.

Just at that moment, a daily newspaper photographer snapped a picture. My first reaction was anger. The photographer was trespassing on a very private moment. When I'd cooled off, I realized that my anger wasn't really caused by the photographer; I was angry that a nice little old lady was dead, that her body was smashed beyond recognition.

The next day the photo of me praying appeared on Page One of the paper. I don't know why I'd been so annoyed with the photographer. He was only doing his job, just like I was doing mine.

The picture won a National Newspaper Award for the photographer, and went around the world. Later, Ottawa Sun photographer Denis Cyr's photo was acclaimed as the Ottawa Sun's Photo of the Decade – 1991-2001. Denis is now Photo Editor of the Toronto Star and very graciously granted me permission to use his award-winning photo for the cover of this book.

The phone calls poured in, praising me for my Christian act. The lady's daughter and son wrote thanking me. I got a few negative calls, but they were from weirdo religious types. The picture went around the world and showed the softer side of a firefighter.

The morgue attendants arrived to remove the body. They put that tiny woman in a zipper bag. They picked her up and were preparing to drop her over a fence because it would mean they wouldn't have to walk too far to their vehicle. That's when I really lost it. I had said my prayers. What I said to the two flunkies couldn't be printed in any respectable journal. I called them every name in the book and told them to handle her remains with dignity. I had two of my men carry her down the track to the body removal truck. I was afraid I might strangle the two insensitive jerks.

Your Services Are No Longer Required

I wish I could say it never happened, but it did. It was the spring of 1974. I entered a burning building and started down the basement stairs. There was hardly any light. I got 15 feet from the stairwell when there was a huge POW. For a split second, everything was clearly illuminated, and then became pitch black. I was under a fridge and stove in total darkness.

I was carried into hospital on a backboard.

I was home, recovering from serious injuries, when I got the news.

A City paper pusher sent me a letter advising me that my services were no longer required. I was injured and unable to work; therefore, I wasn't needed on the voyage.

I was 34 years old. I was a firefighter, and didn't know any other work. I didn't want any other line of work, because I loved my job.

An old Chief once said to me, if you lost your job and went for a job interview, just imagine the dialogue!

Can you just picture me going in for a job interview?

"What do you do, Sir?"

"I'm a firefighter."

"Sorry, we don't have any fires today. What else can you do?"

"I can lead men, inspect your premises for potential fire hazards, check your fire extinguishers, and draw up a fire plan."

"Sorry, what else can you do?" I might as well walk into an interview situation and tell the personnel guy "I'm a Viking" or "I'm a Shepherd".

Anyway, my union/association went to bat for me, my health returned to almost normal and I was allowed back on the job. I was back in a job that made me wake up wet from the neck to the knees. Try as I might I couldn't block out the horror side of it. During the day I could block out the fire, but it always came back to me in my dreams.

Alcohol knocked me out, and for a brief time I could forget. But alcohol was only a crutch; it wasn't a cure. It wasn't the panacea I was looking for.

Alcohol only brought temporary relief and the prospect of permanent problems. It was beginning to affect my home life, as well as my judgement and my senses. I decided I had to get help. I went to a publicly funded addiction foundation, but they didn't know their arses from third base. They pushed pills at me – handfuls of them – hundreds of mood altering chemicals. I was in danger of becoming cross-addicted on pills and booze.

One of the best things that ever happened to me was that I stopped drinking. I'd always been able to cope with whatever the world sent my way, but this was ridiculous. I used to hold down three jobs at the same time – wiring houses for cable TV, playing the drums in local clubs and fighting fires. Now I was hard pressed to do just one. It wasn't until I went to A.A. that things started to turn around for me.

Stopping drinking brought on other problems but they were the lesser of two evils. My drinking bouts in taverns with my buddies were gone. You'd never again see me standing in front of a tavern at 11.50 a.m. waiting for it to open at noon. Fishing and hunting trips were also out, because they were only excuses to leave town and tie one on.

Some Calls Really Get to You

Some calls are really hard to erase from your memory bank. We received a medical call at a big department store. A young employee was pushing cardboard boxes into a shredder, when he slipped and went into the shredder up to his waist.

One of his fellow workmen turned the machine off. We were first on the scene. What a sight.

We called for a doctor and tried to staunch the flow of blood. He lost both his legs below the knees. The doctor had to open his chest and massage his heart. By the Grace of God, he lived.

It still gives me the night sweats. When you sleep, you dream, and some nights you're afraid to go to sleep because you'll awaken your whole family with your screams.

It Takes All Kinds

One of our young guys came into the station all bruised and bloodied. He'd been beaten up pretty badly. I asked him what happened. He said he'd been drinking in a tavern and a waiter and a bouncer kicked the crap out him, without any real provocation.

I went back to the tavern with him that evening, and asked the bouncer if he got his reputation by beating up kids. He said: "I may as well try you, old man."

I dropped him with one punch. He went down like a bag of potatoes. I told his buddy who was trying to grab me: "You take another crack at one of my men and you're next. If you ever kick the shit out of a firefighter again, I'll be back. Touch one of my men and I'll bury the two of you."

A Tracheotomy

A new man came on staff. He was a real know-it-all, a smart-ass son of a bitch. His first day on the job, we responded to a medical call. We didn't have much in the way of training or equipment. All we really had was a Mickey Mouse first aid kit.

Anyway, we ended up saving a guy's life. The know-it-all new guy told me he wasn't too concerned about people having difficulty breathing. He said he had a scalpel inside his fire coat, and if someone was choking to death, he'd cut their throat and stick a straw in.

I said: "Are you out of your fucking mind? What if the guy bleeds to death?"

He answered: "Well, you know, I read a book on it once and I think I'd be pretty good at it."

I said: "Yeah, and then you'll be looking for another job." Shortly afterwards, he was.

How To Make Yourself Unpopular

One of our chums made himself very unpopular. We were working a 24-hour Sunday shift and he brought in his neighbours for a tour around 1 p.m. That was a no-no, because at 1 p.m. on Sundays we were allowed to nap.

They made a helluva racket. He told his neighbours he was going to show them how a fire station responded to an actual fire call.

He went upstairs, put on his fire clothes, and ran towards the fire pole to slide down. He miscalculated and hit the pole with his head. Instead of sliding, he fell down and landed on the floor on his ass. He made a complete fool of himself. It later took four stitches above his eye to close the wound.

Then a real call came in and a bunch of rag tag guys came sliding down the pole in various stages of dress. Must have really impressed the taxpayers.

What's The Phone Number for 911

We received a direct call from a real dopey woman on the fire call phone. We asked her why she didn't phone in on 911.

She said she didn't know the number to call 911. "What's the number?"

An airhead!

Play Ball

Sometimes we went out into the community on public relations appearances. Once we went to a minimum-security prison to play an exhibition baseball game against the inmates. We managed to sneak some beer in for the prisoners, so a good time was had by all. Great PR.

Some of them were just average guys – good guys who went astray. I recognized others from St. Vincent de Paul and Bordeaux penitentiaries. One was a guy I'd had an odd beer with in a hotel on the Quebec side of the Ottawa River.

I got a hit and ended up on second base, where I made small talk with him: "What are you in for?"

He said: "I had trouble with my broad so I murdered her." Lots of class. I'm glad I didn't slide into him making second. I was happier when the next batter advanced me to third.

Smile, You're on Candid Camera

There is one thing that is just not done in a fire station. You never leave a loaded camera around unattended.

One of the rookies left his camera on a table. Some of the guys bent over and mooned while someone else took their pictures. You could only see big hairy arses and their bags hanging down. This young guy's mother-in-law took the film to a camera store to have it developed.

She almost fainted when she saw the photos. She was really impressed! She thought her son-in-law worked with a bunch of degenerates.

Old Firefighter?

I ran into a retired 87-year-old ex firefighter. I asked him what he did with his days.

He answered: "Mondays I bowl, Tuesdays I curl, Wednesdays I go fishing – fly fishing in the summer and ice fishing in the winter, Thursdays I cook for old people".

Cook for old people? 87-years-young and going strong!

Cold Cocked

A 911 call came in, reporting a guy with a knife. We went into his building and there he was, bare-ass naked and holding a huge knife in his hand.

Suddenly, he grabbed his cock and cut it off close to his body. Then he took a swing with the knife and slashed his wrist. He was bleeding like a stuck pig.

By this time, the police had arrived, and a cop came around the corner with a beanbag gun, took a shot at him and hit him in the ribs, intending to slow him down. But it didn't slow him down the way the cop intended. He died.

Oh well, no cock, you might as well be dead anyway.

Nobody's Perfect

A small rural fire department just outside our area wanted to go big city, so they invested in an emergency vehicle. They trained a couple of their guys to man it.

One of the first calls they got was a car accident. The driver of the car was busted up pretty bad.

The attendants put him in the back on a stretcher, but they forgot to lock him in and they didn't lock the back door. They spun their wheels and took off. The poor guy shot out the door onto the main street like he'd been fired out of a cannon. He was really rolling, strapped down, and there wasn't a thing he could do to steer or stop.

The attendants had a pile of shit heaped on them, and were lucky they were able to hang on to their jobs.

Nobody's perfect.

Not One Of The Boys

My transfer to an outlying station wasn't my flavour of the month. The Captain wasn't one of my favourites and he didn't really want me because I was rough around the edges. He was an all-right guy. We just had this personality conflict.

Shortly after I arrived, he advised me: "We have a tradition in this station. We get together on Thursday nights and do a pub-crawl. We have a few pints in different taverns."

I said: "That's a good idea. You continue with your tradition."

"What do you mean? Aren't you joining us?"

I said: "No, I have a tradition. I take my wife out to dinner on Thursdays. That's what I do."

He asked me if I didn't want to be "one of the boys". I told him I was a lone wolf, but would work with him in the fire station and give 110 percent to the job. However, my down time was my own.

Anyway, I've never looked back. I don't feel badly because I wasn't one of the boys. There's a separation between my work place and my home life. My wife and family always came before anything else in the world.

One day I was in a hotel quaffing an ale. I was talking about my wife and children and an elderly gentleman came over and ordered a beer for me.

"What's this for?"

He said he was touched by the way I talked about my wife, and that I must love her very much. He told me he'd just lost his own wife three weeks earlier and a big part of him died along with her.

Another lesson in how we should appreciate something while we have it!

Bless You

An Italian lady rushed into our station in the middle of the afternoon. She was jabbering in Italian, crying, and yelling: "Mamma mia, mamma mia, my baby, she's- a-dying. She cannotta breathe."

She asked me if I was a Catholic and I told her I wasn't but that the Captain, Lornie Watters was.

She insisted that Lornie baptize her baby. She said: "You're the Captain in the fire station. You can do anything!"

So Lornie baptized the baby, in Latin – (I Baptize Thee in the Name of the Father, the Son and the Holy Ghost) and, miracle of miracles, the child started to breathe properly again!

The lady was overcome with relief and gratitude, and Lornie was pretty thrilled himself.

Staying Warm

One of the weirdest calls I ever responded to involved two on-duty cops. It was freezing weather, and they'd found an open side door at a snowmobile and all-terrain vehicle store, so they went in.

There was an ATV parked in the showroom, with the keys in the ignition. They turned the key on and the sucker fired up and somehow slipped into gear.

It bounced off a snowmobile, right out the showroom window and right across the street. It cut off two cars and hit the building on the other side.

They must have done some fancy stick handling to talk themselves out of that fix.

I'll Take Five Boxes

When my daughter Colleen was 10, she was selling Girl Guide cookies, and my wife, Sharon, took her to the fire station on a Saturday afternoon. It was a slow day and the guys were watching a skin flick.

Holy shit, one of the guys leaped over a table and almost killed himself turning off the video.

Colleen told them she was my daughter and that she was selling cookies.

They bought 46 boxes.

Most of her friends only sold five or six.

I guess they thought they'd lose their jobs. My daughter said to my wife a few days later: "Mom, you should have seen the pickle on the man in the movie at the fire station."

Out of the mouth of babes!

Open Sesame

We were responding to a call in a high-rise apartment complex in the middle of winter. We ran into a little old lady in the front lobby, who'd gone in to pick up her girl friend to do some shopping.

She said that when she came back out she couldn't get into her car, because the lock was frozen. Could we help her?

We pulled up alongside her car with the pump and I told one of my men to distract her while I worked on the lock. I went over to the door, peed on the keyhole and turned the key. It worked fine.

The lady said: "My goodness, Sonny, how did you do that?"

I told her it was one of the basic things we were taught in training, and that we were taught to use all sorts of different tools. I didn't tell her I used my one-eyed tool to thaw out her lock.

Meow, Meow

We were kibitzing over lunch at the station, when our Captain complained of heartburn. Someone asked him if he often had problems, and he said there were some things he couldn't digest.

One of the guys turned around and said: "Yeah, like fire hydrants, hoses, telephone poles and cement blocks."

The same Captain had a cat, and he just loved that animal. There was a commercial on TV with cats singing "Meow, Meow, Meow", which he thought was cute, so some of the guys went out behind the station where there was a pay phone and called him.

The nutbars stood there and sang "Meow, Meow, Meow" and then ran back into the station. The Captain wasn't aware they'd slipped out. He put down the phone and said in disgust: "Some idiots just phoned me and started to Meow."

Once, he was hurt at a fire and was asked for his phone number. He said he didn't know what his number was. He just couldn't think of his number.

The nurse said: "Do you even have a phone?" He said he did but couldn't remember the number.

The nurse thought he might be suffering from a concussion. She asked him why he couldn't remember his own phone number.

He said: "There's nothing wrong with me. It's just that I live with a cat and I don't phone the cat or myself, for that matter."

Scum Bags

We got a call to a high-rise in a real nice area of town at about 3:00 a.m. Police were also called for problems in the building. We arrived and were informed that people were trapped in the elevator.

My crew and I started walking up the stairs to find what floor the elevator was stuck on, when we heard a commotion on the fourth. I talked through the door to try and calm the trapped people. I informed them that an elevator repairman was on the way and asked how many were in the elevator and was anybody injured.

A male voice answered: "There are five of us, and the only person who's going to be injured is you, you fat fuck, if you don't get us out of here."

"Watch your tongue, little boy, there are ladies and gentlemen in this building who don't have to hear that kind of filth coming out of your mouth."

"Fuck you, you fat fuck. Open this door and I'll straighten you out."

Those who know me know that's no way to talk to me at any time, and even less at 3:00 a.m. The police arrived. Their information was that five punks, all drunk and drugged up, had broken into the building, looking for something to steal. They got angry and kicked at a few doors on the sixth floor, scaring the residents, who were mostly seniors. Then they got on the elevator and started punching buttons and the elevator got stuck between the 3rd and 4th floors.

The police officer who'd joined us was a tough fellow, who came from a big family and the wrong side of the tracks. He said to me, "Jimmy, when the door opens, handle it any way you want to. We're not garbage and no one has the right to talk to us with such disrespect."

The rest of the police officers had been sent to the 6th floor to calm down the terrified seniors. On the scene was the remaining police officer, two of my guys and me.

The elevator door opened and I said in a calm voice, "Which one of you pukes wants a piece of this fat fuck?" All of a sudden there was silence. I grabbed a guy by the throat who was getting ready to take a punch at me. He croaked to the police officer, "Help me". His answer: "You said you wanted a piece of the fat fuck, so go for it punk." I think he shit his pants. My guys were waiting for one of the other four to make a move, and they would have taken care of that situation for me. A paddy wagon was called for the five of them, who were handcuffed and shackled. I then made their morning by suggesting to the police officer that until their court appearance at 10:00 a.m., they should be put in jail with the general population, letting it be known that they had terrified a group of seniors. There are lots of decent people in jail, and if there's one thing that they don't like it's punks that would terrify senior citizens.

I hope that made their morning. It certainly made mine.

Medical Calls

We get lots of medical calls. Some are tragic, some are scary and some are downright funny.

We were called to a single family home. The lady who met us had a distraught look on her face. She told us she'd rented a third floor room to an elderly gentleman to supplement her modest pension. She hadn't seen or heard from him in a couple of days and was worried.

She let us into his room. What a sad and strange sight. There was a shape under a sheet – like a shroud. Our Captain took the sheet off and revealed an elderly man's body. His eyes were wide open. He had a book in one hand and the other hand was over his heart. I don't know why, but I guess the sheet was over his head when the heart attack hit him.

The police and the coroner arrived within minutes. Rigor mortis had already set in. The body removal team knew it was going to have a problem straightening the body and negotiating the winding stairs.

About twenty curious neighbours – men, women and children – were gathered on the lawn. Fire trucks and emergency vehicles are always natural magnets.

The body removal people had to break the old man's bones to lay him down flat. It was not a pretty sight and the sound effects weren't pleasant either.

We were carrying the litter down the front steps when all Hell broke loose. The restraining chest strap broke and the body shot forward. His eyes were wide open, and one arm swung forward and scared the living shit out of the people on the grass.

I will never forget their screams, especially those of the children. Those kids will take that sight to their graves.

Love and Marriage

It takes a special breed of woman to marry a firefighters. Shift work is murder on family life. Wives wonder if their husbands will come home all beaten to rat-shit – or drunk. Sometimes, they must wonder if they'll come home alive at all.

There are positive sides to shift work – not many – but there are some, one of which is breezing through a supermarket because you're the only person in the store.

I always tell people: "I know I'm not the sharpest knife in the drawer." That's why I was slow on the uptake when neighbours stopped me on the street and pulled my wire. If I'd been quicker on the draw I'd have asked them what the Hell they were doing home themselves at that time of the day.

I was lucky. My wonderful wife Sharon's father was a police detective, so she didn't have to make any adjustments when she married me. Her Dad worked shifts too.

I think she liked it when I pulled the 24-hour stint. She could get caught up with her chores and her reading, as well as visiting with her friends.

One firefighter I worked with was having marital problems. His wife hated his broken workweek and she never let him forget it. One Monday morning, after a 24-hour Sunday shift, he went home, and the only things left in his house were a table and chair, a bowl, a cup and saucer and a knife and fork. He was devastated. He came back to the station and I could tell right away there was something wrong. We went out to the apparatus floor and sat at the back near the hose tower.

I asked him if he had a problem. I told him he looked like he had the weight of the world on his shoulders. He was fighting back tears. My heart went out to him.

It might have been different if he'd been abusive or a piss tank but he was an all around nice guy.

Anyway, he got down on his knees and begged her to come home. They went for counselling and tried to start over, but six months later she left him again.

My Dad always told me that tensions between men are best eased by duking it out and then going for a beer. Women are different. They're smaller, and they pack a different kind of punch. Get them angry, and you're bound to lose. Look at the Falkland Islands when they pissed off Margaret Thatcher.

We Have an "Unknown" High Rise Call

Our dispatcher sent us off to a call from a high rise. The problem was "unknown". It could be a jumper, a suicide, a fire, a murder or a drowning. But this one turned out to be different.

We look an elevator to the sixteenth floor and walked up one flight. It was daytime, with rain and thunder crashing outside. We knocked on the door of the apartment from which the call had originated. A rude asshole answered and said: "What took you so long?"

Our Captain was ex-military and programmed to be an officer and a gentleman, but don't talk to him in a nasty tone of voice unless you want to start brushing your teeth through your asshole.

"What's your problem? Do you have a fire? An injury?"

The guy started screaming at the Captain: "Water is coming through my ceiling." The Captain's back was up so he told him to call maintenance. The fellow kept screaming that water was coming through his ceiling and he wanted us to clean it up.

The Captain was really blowing steam, and he started backing the guy towards the balcony. The complainant, who by now was getting intimidated and a little nervous, demanded: "What's your name? What's your badge number?" The Captain took off his helmet and showed him the nameplate, all the while continuing to advance.

Holy fuck, I thought he was going to throw the rude bastard off the balcony. The jerk said he was going to get in touch with the newspapers.

I went over to the Captain and told him it wasn't worth it, so he finally said to the puke: "Fuck you" and walked out. It was that rude prick's lucky day he got off that easy.

For King and Country

I chatted with an old retired firefighter in a pub one afternoon. He said he'd done it all and had few, if any, regrets. He believed his country needed him in the Second World War, so he lied about his age and went off to fight.

He said it was rough, very rough, but that it made a man out of him very quickly, and that the things he had seen and done still preyed on his mind. There were still times when he'd wake up in the middle of the night, drenched in sweat. It didn't matter if it was winter or summer. Sometimes, his nightmares scared him so much he pissed the bed.

He said modern shrinks don't refer to his nightmares as night sweats or shell shock any more. The new buzz phrase is traumatized.

"It's all the same shit. Just a different day!"

He came home from the war with an English war bride, and they had 49 happy years together. He lost her just as they were looking forward to their fiftieth anniversary. Cancer took her away from him, and he missed her terribly, but felt that she was in a far better place. They'd had five children. Three were still alive. One was killed crossing a street and another died from polio.

Then he said: "Look at me. I've been shot at, blown up, taken prisoner, beaten and spit on by the enemy. Two of my children died before they were old enough to live."

After the war he joined the fire department – long hours and not the best paying job. He had no regrets. He said that, like me, he'd worked with many different men, and although none were rocket scientists, we loved our country and our jobs, just as he did.

He despised some men. He called them the Two-Y Club – too young to fight in World War 1 and too yellow to fight in World War II.

He said he'd be gone soon, but every time he looked in the mirror a man looked back at him – not a draft dodging gutless bastard.

Three months later he was gone!

One Mouth, Two Ears

God gave us one mouth and two ears. Right off the bat, this should tell you to listen twice as much as you talk. I love people, and I love to talk. To my credit, I'm also a good listener.

I have a very kind nature and my heart always reacts the right way. When I know a person's hurting, I try to persuade them to let it all out. The things I respect most are family, country, the military, policemen and firefighters. I often thought it would be neat to sculpt a composite statue of all these elements. I love having long talks with retired military and emergency services veterans. Most of them suffered silently during their careers.

One old guy told me that nothing changes in this world. I said: "Sure, it does!" He said there were three things you couldn't do, and would never change. I asked him what they were.

He said you can't satisfy everybody. You can't educate the unwashed and you can't get everybody to like you. He said after his wife died he gave his daughter $100,000 and his son $50,000. The son was suing him for more, even though he never had any time for him. He said we would never have had a Second World War if we could have educated the masses and learned from the first war. As far as people went, they could dislike you for many reasons – your accent, your personality, because you're talkative, the colour of your skin, etc.

Live and let live. Be good to yourself. Stand up for yourself. He was a wise old man who packed a lot of living and learning into his 88 years.

Crack!
(Heron Road Bridge)

CRACK!

I never heard a sound like it before or since. It was early one sunny afternoon. Three of us were standing in front of the fire station.

What the hell was that crack? It couldn't possibly be a sonic boom or we would have been knocked down. It was not unlike the sound of a huge branch being broken away from a large oak tree – only a hundred times louder. Then an all stations call came in. A bridge under construction collapsed under a load of wet cement and reinforcing rods.

Get your gear on and get going!

We were on the scene in minutes. Every emergency organization in the city responded. I would never experience another day like this in my entire career. The scene was like a snapshot of Dante's Inferno – only worse.

Tons of fresh, quick drying cement were imprisoning scores of workmen in a river gorge. One workman had an iron rod through his body. He was bleeding to death, and begging for a priest.

Another man was up to his hips in wet cement. He was crying and screaming in a foreign tongue. We were trying to extricate another man from the soup and he was traumatized, in pain, and babbling. Legs and arms and dead bodies were all over the twisted wreckage. I never felt so helpless in all my life.

Grown men were crying like babies. There were broken bones, broken spirits and broken hearts. The tortured living were envying the dead.

Our shift was over at 5:00 p.m. but we stayed there until 11:30. We did the best we could but, in many cases, it was hopeless. It was a horror show. Nine workmen died.

One fellow was trapped beneath a dead man. In order to extricate him, the doctors had to amputate one of the dead man's legs.

What a job. What a life. What a picture of horror and terror. It's part of what we do and we do our best. My God, have you any idea what it's like to work with the calibre of men I've worked with for over 39 years?

I've been truly blessed.

Get Out Of Here, You Bastard

My Captain, Keith Tucker, was in hospital, having his appendix removed.

I went to visit him and he said: "Get out of here, you bastard, and don't come back. I'll get even with you."

He said this with a smile on his face. What did I do? I made him laugh. He had lots of stitches and he didn't want a nutbar like me making him laugh.

His roommate was a very prim and proper 55-year-old school teacher wearing horn rim glasses. He wouldn't say shit if he had a mouthful.

I had them both in tears and that's when Keith threw me out. A month later, he was back at work and he pointed his crooked finger at me.

"You son-of-a-bitch. You should have been a stand-up comedian."

I said: "Come on, Captain, you love me like a son, don't you?"

He said: "I love all of you bunch of screw-ups."

Another time, he came out into the kitchen area and announced: "I lost my wedding ring."

Twenty minutes later, after looking around his office, he came back out and said: "I found the ring. I'm so relieved. I didn't want my wife to kill me."

I asked: "Where did you find it, Captain?"

He said: "In my office bed."

My response: "Was it crushed?"

"You bastard."

Captain Keith was a big man, well over 250 pounds.

I Was Injured

I got racked up and for a while it looked like my injuries were serious enough to force me to change jobs.

I looked around, and attended a few self-help seminars. All around me were suits and plastic. I took some counselling, but when the group found out I was a firefighter, I became the centre of attention.

Everybody wanted this oddity at his table. One of the men told me he thought I was the only non-plastic person in the room. He was amazed I would want to swap my career for something else. Someone else asked me to be a guest on his TV program and talk about firefighting, which I said I'd be happy to do. After the show aired, he phoned Sharon who was crying and asked: "Where did he get his training? That was the best show I ever did." She replied, "He has no formal training, except that he knows and loves his job." God bless my Sharon.

I will bet a month's pension that salesmen and other white-collar workers don't get stopped in shopping malls and given big hugs by complete strangers. The uniform does it every time.

Buy Me a Box of .32 Bullets

I was visiting a real old retired firefighter in a nursing home. He had terminal cancer but retained a great attitude. The man who shared his room looked too young to be in a nursing home. He was only about 45.

He asked me how I would like to make $10,000. I asked him who he wanted killed.

He was very depressed and started to cry. He pulled back the blanket, raised his hospital gown and showed me his naked body. His penis and testicles had been surgically removed because of cancer. He said his wife had left him, cleaned out their bank account but missed his safety deposit box.

He said he had $10,000 and a .32 calibre pistol in the box. He wanted me to get the gun and buy him a box of bullets. He said he only needed one. He told me the money would be mine.

I couldn't do it. He begged me. He said no one would ever know. Wrong! I would know.

He died from his cancer a few months later.

Somebody Up There Didn't Like Me

I had an officer who, for some reason, didn't like me. Maybe it was because I flunked the Dale Carnegie course. Maybe it was because he flunked the Dale Carnegie course.

After 10 years as a firefighter, I was eligible to write exams to qualify to be a junior officer. I never considered myself a scholar. Studying for exams was not my bag. Neither was writing them. As if that wasn't bad enough, I had to be rated by an officer who didn't like me.

In spite of everything, I was really pleased with my results on the written exam. I was even more pleased but dumbfounded when my officer gave me perfect ratings.

I asked to see him in his office. I said that right off the top I wanted to thank him for the great rating. I said it came as a surprise because we had personality clashes.

He said: "You're so right, Jimmy. I don't like you. You're mouthy and arrogant."

That stung, so I tried to deal with the part about being mouthy. I told him I came from a family of 13, where you had to be mouthy to be heard, but that I tried to get along with people. As for being arrogant, I wasn't that at all. I just had a lot of self-confidence, and have always been good to my family, friends and people I work with.

Then he said something I have never forgotten: "Look, whether I like you or not doesn't mean a thing. I respect you. You're a good man, an excellent firefighter and you do as you're told. You keep the station running and you have a gift that enables you to deal with the public. It's more important to be respected than to be liked."

Different Strokes

Firefighters have to deal with many different support agencies – police, ambulance, the military, the gas company and hydro. In the event of a major fire, even the bus company is alerted. If it's cold or wet we might need empty buses, so homeless fire victims have a place to shelter.

You meet a lot of people dealing with so many agencies, and some become friends. There was a hydro crew who'd park their truck behind our fire hall and came in to have coffee with us. One of the hydro workers was a particularly nice man. He was 6'4", weighed around 260, and we got on really well together.

I was transferred to another station, and didn't see him for a couple of years. When I was transferred back, one of the first people I met was him. He had lost 100 pounds, but I recognized him by his broad smile.

His once bright complexion was a chalky grey and he was gaunt. He told me he had the big "C". We had a coffee and hugged each other. Two hours later we got a call to a hydro station. He had gone up a catwalk and jumped into the hydro vault. He died instantly.

Our Life Blood

Let's face it! Whether we like it or not, gas and oil are what make the world go round. Until we find an alternative fuel they're our lifeblood. They make the country tick.

Gas and oil are also a firefighter's main enemies. If they're stored improperly, it could be game over. During an energy crisis, people were doing the stupidest things. They were hoarding gasoline and storing it everywhere except under their beds.

We responded to hundreds of calls because somebody smelled gasoline. In one instance, two of our men were looking for the source of a gas smell in a basement.

One of them found a big flat tray of gas. It was being used to clean motorcycle parts. He'd started to carry the tray across the floor to take it up the stairs and outside, when it exploded.

The furnace had kicked in, and the air/gas mix was right. He lit up like a Roman candle. Gas got in his boots and his legs were also badly burned.

You had two firefighters finding out what Hell was like. Their screams were like something out of a Grade B horror flick. Both of them were on fire. Thank God they had their helmets on and their ear lugs down or they would have lost their hair and ears.

The flames got under their fire coats, and their pants and underwear caught fire. They were rushed to the burn centre and immersed in a saline solution. They had second and third degree burns to their private parts, and were hospitalized for more than a month. They were so badly burned, it was hard to find whole skin for grafts.

One good thing came out of that horror show. The City invested in new full-body fire suits to better protect us.

Hazmat

Since I retired, the role of the firefighter has taken on yet another dimension – dealing with hazardous materials (Hazmat). Fire departments have always had to deal with noxious materials, but these substances were not in the hands of terrorists then.

Terrorism in Canada is a relatively new phenomenon. We saw it first in 1970 when ultra-nationalists in Quebec kidnapped a British diplomat, killed a Quebec Cabinet Minister, and began booby-trapping mailboxes.

We had no inkling then of what lay ahead. We had no idea that terrorism would spill across national borders. We had no way of knowing that terrorists halfway around the world were targeting our way of life and our population.

The horror of 9/11 in New York was and still is mind-boggling. What possible cause is served by killing innocent civilians? What message is being sent when a federal building in Oklahoma is blown up, killing almost 300 people?

The tools that terrorists have in their arsenals are frightening. One of the Hazmat experts told me that using $300 worth of everyday chemicals and a rental cube truck, he could take out a major embassy. He also said he could kill 1,000 people in an office building in just seconds.

Terrorism has brought the civilized world closer together. My fire department is no longer an island unto itself. It's been thrust into contact with most of the major police, fire and emergency services in the world. It's cooperating on a daily basis with all of the United States' Homeland Security agencies.

I was born, raised and have lived my life as a Christian. My religion taught me to have respect for others. I cannot comprehend how or why some other religions invoke the name of their higher power to wage war on, and kill, innocent victims.

We are now faced with indiscriminate, wanton attacks by suicide killers who do not hesitate to use explosives, bacteria, chemicals or even nuclear devices to achieve their goals. What are their goals, I ask? What religion promotes such hatred?

Hazmat is the elite group of firemen who have their fingers in the dike. They're the ones who are called upon when suspicious materials are found. They're the shock troops who have to remove the material and dispose of it.

They operate under one severe handicap. They have no way of knowing where or when.

After the attack on Pearl Harbour, U.S. President Franklin Roosevelt said, "The only thing we have to fear is fear itself." If we give in to fear, the terrorists have won a major battle – a major battle, but not the war.

What a Way To Go

I talked to an old firefighter once, who told me how his father died. I said it must have been tragic to lose him.

He said: "No, my Dad died the way he lived. He had a good time."

I asked him how he died and he told me.

"He was 77 years old and retired. He was down in Daytona Beach in Florida, driving his Harley Davidson motorcycle along the beach. On the back seat, he had a dental floss bikini hooker. He had a massive heart attack, ran into a cement abutment and was killed instantly. He died like he lived."

If you have to die you might as well go out in style. So now I have myself a new hero. Maybe when it's time to go, I'll be on a Harley.

In life, LIVE. Don't just exist. Travel. Do things. Life's too short. Do it now. You may not get a second chance.

9/11

I sat for almost an entire day in front of my TV set. I experienced more emotion than I ever had before in my life. Early morning, Sept. 12th, 2001, I phoned the Chief of the Ottawa Fire Department, Tommy Blondin, and asked him what we were going to do to help.

He said that they were making a list. I asked him to put my name on the list, and he said he couldn't because I had the same heart condition he had and I might die if I went.

I did my bit, donated to the families, but I never felt like it was enough. I ran into one of my men and he told me he had spent two weeks of his holidays helping, as he said, "in the hole in New York." I asked him if he could get me the names of the men who went to help. He did and I phoned each one and told them how very proud I was of them and that I loved and respected them all. If it's God's will, and I write a second book, I'm going to write a story about each of these men. They were told not to go but they went anyway, because they knew in their heart of hearts that it was the right thing to do.

* * * * * * * * * * *

One day, another one of my neighbours who always jerked me around grabbed me in a bear hug. I was taken aback. I didn't know what was going on. He had tears in his eyes. He said: "Until September 11 in New York, I never realized what you did for a living. My opinion of firefighters was that you were the only group of people besides hookers who got paid so much money for spending so much time in bed."

That moment, that hug, those words made almost four decades of flirting with danger and death all seem worthwhile.

People are entitled to their opinions but firefighters know what they do for a living and they don't have to apologize for anything or to anybody.

Millionaire's Club

Earlier this year I was in Nassau, Bahamas, and thanks to Sharon's cousin Heather d'Albenas, we had access to places we would never have otherwise been able to get into. We were invited to a club in Lyford Cay – really a club for the ultra rich. While there, I heard a man's scream and followed the sound to see what the problem was. A male was down on the tennis court, and I went toward him.

A man got in front of me and blocked my access to the fallen man. I pushed him gently out of my way and this pissed him off. He said to me gruffly: "Are you a doctor or something?" I answered: "I'm better than that, I'm a firefighter." That pissed him off, too. Ask me if I cared. I got down and worked on the injured man. It turned out it wasn't a heart attack. It was only a knee injury and everything worked out well. Your chances of living are as good or better with a trained firefighter as with a doctor. Why? In this litigation-happy world doctors are afraid of being sued for malpractice.

In most cases, a doctor will try to find a pulse and lose vital seconds. A firefighter will do the five basic things automatically… breathing, bleeding, shock, stabilization and comfort. This is why your chances are so much better with a firefighter than a doctor. I have done mouth to mouth or in some cases mouth to nose. It's just another orifice to breathe into and it works, especially on children. Of the 11 people I worked on, 10 lived.

The bottom line is the taxpayers do get one hell of a bang for their buck and if it ain't broke, don't fix it. Of course, as with anything in this book, it's my personal opinion, and, in a free country, I have the right to free thought and the right to express it.

Sir Sean Connery and Sheila Hailey

On a trip to Nassau, a couple of years ago, I managed to get Arthur and Sheila Hailey's address, as well as Sean Connery's. On my return to Ottawa I wrote them letters about what I was trying to do, pertaining to my book. Sheila Hailey was kind enough to write me a long letter, and informed me that her husband was ill. He has since passed away. The world lost a great man and writer. He went into the Air Force in England from 1939-1945, and served in Canada from 1946-1958, working out of the old Rockcliffe Air Base and Trenton. He served both countries very honorably. I have kept in touch with Sheila. Such a classy lady.

* * * * * * * * * * *

When we went to Nassau earlier this year, Sheila phoned me at Heather and Robert's home to inform us that the dinner plans we'd made had to be cancelled because her sister had died in England, and she was going there the following morning for the wake and funeral. We'd get together another time.

* * * * * * * * * * *

Sean Connery had the respect to phone me in March of 2004. I thought it was someone playing a trick on me until he mentioned things that I had written in my letter to him. I asked if I could visit him on our next holiday to Nassau. He answered "Please do."

On February 16, 2005, I drove to Sean Connery's house. If you look up the word gentleman in the dictionary, I'm sure his picture is there next to it. Such a wonderful person! I asked him if I could write a story about him and use his picture. He said "Most assuredly."

Sir Sean has property in New York and saw the evil, horror and devastation of 9/11 first hand. He felt, as many others did, when watching the firefighters enter the building, that they weren't coming out. They died in the line of duty, nobly serving their country.

And we must never forget them. Why? Because if you forget the past you're doomed to relive it.

I have always tried to stand tall as a firefighter. These men help me stand even taller. Sir Sean's empathy towards firefighters is what prompted me to put his picture on the back of this book.

I asked Sir Sean if he would play the Fire Chief, if my book was successful and made into a movie. I told him he'd look great in a Chief's coalscuttle helmet. His eyebrows arched. He didn't say yes but he didn't say no either. The bottom line goes back to my dear old dad who said to me, and I know he meant it: "Jimmy, the bigger they are, the nicer they are."

These two icons proved my Dad right.

Injuries

During a conversation with my friend and mentor, Pat MacAdam, he asked about the injuries I'd sustained fighting fires. I never thought much about it because I figured it was the price I had to pay to be a firefighter.

That night, while laying in bed, I started thinking about it. Being a firefighter in 1960 was not like it is today. Back in the 60's masks were rare, and even then, the older guys didn't like wearing them. They couldn't get used to them. It took me a couple of years to get accustomed to a mask.

Fighting fires is much like riding a Harley. At first, you're hyper cautious, then you get sloppy and stupid, and then if you're not dead you get to the point where your training kicks in, and everything comes together. That's when your chances of living improve.

In the 1960's our equipment was very basic – axes, pike poles, sledge hammers. We weren't issued safety goggles or gloves. Stitches from cuts and abrasions, dislocated shoulders, broken arms and legs were everyday occurrences.

When you entered a burning structure – no mask and very little protection – accidents happened. You stayed close to the floor and tried to find some air. When you found a window you broke it, punching it out with your hose key, your elbow or with a woolen mitt that provided little or no protection. It was hell! With auto accidents, we used whatever we had on hand. After all, we were only firefighters as far as City Hall was concerned.

This attitude still holds today. Some of the junk we have for fire trucks would never pass a Department of Transport test, if someone in the private sector owned them. Even our fire stations, built in the 1960's, were built without air conditioners because the City didn't feel we were worth it. At our station, all four shifts pitched in and bought our own units, giving us some comfort from the heat of the flat tar roofs.

Back to my injuries. As I remember, some of them were life threatening. I've had at least four concussions, cracked vertebrae in my neck, and four compressed discs in my back from an explosion in a warehouse. I was knocked off a beam and fell 10-12 feet on my face. My air mask hit me on the back of my neck and head. I was forced to lay motionless until a doctor was summoned to check me out. In the same fall I cracked a kneecap, loosened some teeth and dislocated both shoulders.

Over the years I dislocated my left shoulder five times and my right one four times. My left eye was almost pulled out of its socket by a druggie during a fire call. At least three times I had to have my eyes washed out and chemicals or bits of glass flushed out. I got eight stitches above my left eye. I could actually see through my eyelid. I had a cracked cheekbone. I burned both ears fighting a fire in an old house. I was up three stories and on the end of a ladder when a glob of hot tar landed on the back of my gloveless right hand. It was either take the pain, try to wipe the tar off on your fire coat, or fall off the ladder and maybe get maimed or killed.

I broke my left leg below the knee. Today, I'm a candidate for two new knees. Both my ankles are shot. My right ankle is bigger than the left by at least an inch.

When you're 20 years old, fighting fires without an air mask, and in your first winter on the job you deal with 17 deaths, a whole lot of damage is done inside your head.

My Colleagues, Friends and Heroes

Nookie

One of the nicest characters in my Grade "B" movie type life was Nookie. A real great guy and lots of fun. We went to high school together until he dropped out, and then I lost track of him. He did some reform school time for some break and enters and other stupid things. I ran into him; he was glad to see me and we had a few beers together. I asked him "Nookie, what are you going to do with your life? You're very smart and could turn your hand to anything."

His answer stunned me. "I'm going to be a career criminal."

"What?" I asked.

"Yes, my uncle Tony is one. His house is paid for, he has a cottage and a winter home in Florida." He continued, saying, "Jimmy, reform school is high school and Kingston Pen is university."

"What the hell do you mean, Nookie?"

"Look, Jimmy. I'm going to court for passing some paper (cheques). I want to get sent to Kingston so I can learn how to be a Pete man."

"What the hell is a Pete man, Nookie?"

"That's what my uncle Tony is. A Pete man is slang for a safe cracker. My uncle can file his finger tips down and feel the tumblers going into place in the safe door. I want to learn how it's done and other ways of getting into safes."

Nookie was a real nice, non-violent man, and when he went to court the judge didn't want to send him to Kingston. He wanted to send him to a safer place like reform school. When asked if he had anything to say before being sentenced, Nookie said, "Your Honor, all I ever learned in reform school was to cut pigs' throats."

The judge said "Okay, smart guy… three years in Kingston Pen." Just what Nookie wanted!

Every once in awhile, when I was in Kingston wiring buildings for television in the early stages of cablevision in the 1960's (my sideline job), I would visit him along with other friends in prison. I asked him "What's it like in here Nookie?"

"Like I said one time, Jimmy, it's university. We'll talk more when I get out."

When he got out he really put what he'd learned to use and made lots of money knocking off safes in chain stores and drug stores. The great alarm and closed circuit TV surveillance systems were not available in the 1960's. Nookie would open a roof vent and lower himself down, open the safe and go back up the rope. He made a shit load of cash and to justify what he was doing he would tell me "I hurt no one, I'm non-violent. I know I'll get caught eventually but as I say, I hurt no one." Oh, the criminal mind is so very complex.

I ran into Nookie about a year later. He looked fit and healthy. Heh, if you're lowering yourself through a hole in the roof via rope you have to be fit and in shape. We were leaving a downtown hotel together when he said to me: "Jimmy, that really pisses me off."

"What does?" I questioned.

"Look across the street in that window. There's a big Taylor safe and it must be 3 ft. high and 4 ft. wide and about 4 ft. deep."

"So what's the problem, Nookie?"

"It's a big safe and I couldn't work on it in the window. I'd have to figure a way to get it out of there."

"You're kidding!" I said.

"Watch me", he said.

About a month later I read that a big Taylor safe was stolen out of a building in downtown Ottawa. I started to laugh until I had tears in my eyes. I had to find out how the hell he did it. Nookie left town and went south for a few weeks. When he came home, he visited me at the fire hall with a tan and a big smile on his face. We went and sat in the kitchen and I put on the coffee. No one except he and I were in the room.

"Ok, you bastard", I said laughingly. "How did you do it? How?"

"It was really easy", he said. "I stole a half-ton truck about 50 miles outside of Ottawa. I hid it for a couple of weeks. I put Acme Safe Company signs onto each door. I got a smock and had Acme Safe Company embroidered on it. I drove to the business. The big safe was about 500 lbs., ("less when I emptied it", he laughed). I had a ramp I'd built and you know from my past I can get into any building. I went in the front, rolled the safe to the door and got it out on the sidewalk in front of the building. You know, Jimmy, I'm strong but not that heavy, and I couldn't push the safe up into the truck. I damn near crippled myself. What the hell was I going to do? Then an idea hit me. I walked up to Bank Street, saw a very big beat cop and said to him: 'Could you help me please, sir?' The cop asked me how he could be of assistance. I told him, 'My name is Ralph and I work for Acme Safe Company, and I'm not very big as you can see. My partner took sick and went home before I could finish moving a safe. I got it out on the street but I can't push it up the company truck ramp. Would you help me, officer? We working men have to stick together and I don't want to phone my boss at 2.30 a.m. for assistance.'

'I know what you mean' he replied.

We went back to the safe. I was shaking like a dog shitting icicles. With this fine officer's help the safe went up the ramp and into the box of the truck very easily. His last words to me were 'make sure you tie that safe down so it won't roll off the truck.'

'No problem, officer.'

Then he walked back to his beat. I took the safe to a garage a few miles out of town and opened it. Those old Taylor safes are easy to open. All you have to do is get a wheel-puller, put it over the tumblers, drill three holes and pull off the dial with the wheel-puller. There are three pins. Use a chisel and a hammer. Knock two outside pins down and the center one up and the door swings open."

The newspapers had fun with this story. The beat cop must have had a hard time explaining his role.

Oh, the wonderful, helpful things Nookie learned in the crow bar motel!

Johnny

In 1965, Johnny Harrison (who was one of my best friends and a brother firefighter) and I, were talking to a couple of Americans over a couple of beers and they asked us what we did for a living. We, of course, were very proud to tell them we were firefighters.

They asked: "Have you ever thought of going overseas to fight fires?" Johnny said: "Never!"

We were told the American government was hiring trained firefighters to go to different countries around the world on two-year contracts. They were offering danger pay and after two years service, U.S. citizenship. It tweaked our interest. Johnny and I were both proud Canadians but we were also very pro-American.

We soon realized it wouldn't work. The first place we'd be sent would be Vietnam, and Johnny said we'd probably get ourselves killed. We dropped that idea.

Life has many strange twists and turns. Johnny died March 7, 1969, in a major fire. He was only 31.

He was a good man and a great friend. I guess Johnny is getting his answers in the next world – not this one. I was lucky to have him for my friend – even for so short a time.

Gerry

Another of my firefighting buddies was Gerry. He was a great guy and came from the same type of background that I did. Gerry and I had something else in common – alcohol, and it caused us many problems throughout our lives. When I found Alcoholics Anonymous, Gerry tried it out and found it wasn't for him. Because I quit going to taverns, we drifted apart.

Gerry had another addiction which turned out to be deadly – gambling. As most people know, drinking and thinking are not synonymous. Gerry loved to drink and gamble. He was out of his league in a matter of months, and owed about $5,000.

Remember, this was the early 1970's and $5,000 was a whole shit load of money. Bankers tell us that the purchasing power of money doubles every seven years, so go figure. Along with losing his job, having a drinking problem and a gambling addiction, he also had heart trouble.

Late one night he got a knock on the door and it was two hoods from Montreal, looking for their $5,000. He told them he didn't have it and that he'd lost his job. One of them said: "Look Mac, if you're looking for sympathy, look in the dictionary between sex and syphilis. We'll be back in two weeks and you now owe the man $6,000 and you better have it! Understand?"

Three days later Gerry ended up in the hospital for open-heart surgery, which was a big deal back then. After the operation, some of his so-called buddies sneaked him in some alcohol. Was the doctor ever pissed off! In the meantime, two weeks had passed and the hoods informed him by phone that his bill was now $7,000 and to have it ready.

A few days later, when Gerry was released from the hospital, he got right back into the booze, and about 2 a.m. the hoods came back looking for their money.

Gerry opened his shirt to show them he was cut from his neck to his belly button. The hoods could see his scar. One of them hit Gerry an unexpected sucker punch in the middle of the chest. Gerry was dead in two hours… God rest his soul.

Eddie

One of the nicest older Captains I worked under was Eddie. He was ex-military. He enlisted when he was 17 because he believed "if a country is good enough to live in, it's good enough to fight for." He was unlike a lot of other gutless bastards who ducked service over the years.

When Captain Eddie came into the fire hall there was an aura about him. He stood out. His uniform was a cut above everyone else's. His shirt was crisply starched and bluer than blue. The crease in his trousers and the spit and polish on his shoes, made everyone sit up and take notice. It was an honour and a privilege to be directed by a man of his courage and dignity.

Soon after he retired he complained of headaches. When he came to visit us at the fire hall you could tell he was in pain, but he never complained. When he didn't show up for a few days I phoned. His wife answered the phone and she was crying.

She said Eddie had a stroke and might not live. He lost the sight of his left eye, his speech was slurred and the muscles along his left side were affected.

His wife told me: "He can't even shave himself."

My heart went out to her. She said, "His will to live isn't there anymore. All he ever lived for was his family, his country, his military life and his fire department. He's so dependent and so depressed."

My brother firefighters and I took him to therapy and visited him in his home, but the spark was gone. He was in and out of hospital and it looked like his future would be inside a nursing home.

One sunny Wednesday afternoon just after noon there was a faint knock on the door of the fire hall. Nobody knocks on the door of a fire hall. People just walk in. We didn't even have locks until the 1960s and then only because some pukes would steal in and boost our wallets and shoes.

I went to the door and opened it. It was Captain Eddie. He was one of the saddest sights I have ever seen. He had a three-day growth of beard and was wearing a baggy old pair of fire department pants and shoes. He had lost over 50 pounds and had a sad, hangdog look on his face. I almost cried.

We all made a big fuss over him and fed him lunch. At 1:30 our new Captain told us to get ready to hit the streets to inspect houses.

Captain Eddie said he'd be OK alone. His wife was coming at 2 p.m. to pick him up. He thanked us for lunch and said he'd see us again real soon.

When we finished our inspections we returned to the fire hall, and one of the rookies ran upstairs to take a leak. Seconds later we heard a God awful yell. We ran upstairs, thinking the kid had hurt himself or something. He was standing in the bedroom looking down in terror at a dead man.

Captain Eddie had an empty pill bottle by his side. He left a scribbled suicide note that said: "I can't go on. Please forgive me. Eddie."

I cried buckets that afternoon.

Ernie

One of the men I had the pleasure of working with was Ernie – a real hero in my eyes. When he was only 18, he went off to war without hesitation. He carried his respect for the uniform from the Army to the Fire Department. He took pride in his uniform and taught me how to spit and polish my shoes.

Ernie and some of the Second World War and Korean War vets would stand while they drank their morning coffee. I finally asked them why? The answer was they didn't want to wrinkle the crease in their trousers. Such respect for the uniform! They would get just as dirty as the rest of us when the gong hit.

A few years later I was working with Ernie, who was then a Captain. The City had just hired its first firefighter of Middle Eastern descent. His family was so proud that their son was a firefighter.

One Sunday morning we handled a real dirty stove fire. Stove-pipes, soot and garbage from the ceiling fell on us. We knocked the fire down and returned to the station.

Captain Ernie said: "I'm going to take a shower. You guys get dinner on and get the rigs ready for the next call."

Ernie was a gentleman's gentleman, but he liked to play like the rest of us. After his shower Ernie, bare balls and all, ran into the visiting area, jumped up in the air, clicked his heels and farted. My God, what a sight! The young Arab had invited his grand-father, grandmother, his father and mother, two of his sisters and three of his brothers to the fire station to meet all his wonderful fire fighting brothers and his first Captain. What the hell could you say? How could you explain a performance like that?

The parents looked at each other. Their mouths dropped open, and grandma almost lost her burka

Ernie wanted to open his wrists with a dull spoon.

Paul

You couldn't ask for a better mate than Paul. He was one of the nicest men I ever worked with. He was lots of fun, a good drinking buddy and great to fight fires with.

He was a few years older than me and on our days off, we would get together once in a while.

Paul started losing weight. He thought it was cancer from all the shit we ingested and breathed in over the years. His weight dropped from 220 to 170 pounds in two months, and he was really becoming concerned.

One of the older firemen told him to go and get himself checked out for diabetes, and when he did, the results were positive. It was this disease that was making him waste away.

His doctor told him "no more alcohol". He tried to quit but couldn't. One morning, he was really hung over and he went into the barbershop for a shave and a haircut. He'd been on a bender for three days, hadn't shaved, and was feeling pretty sick.

He sat in the barber's chair. The barber, a nice old Italian guy named Tony, had a weird sense of humour. Paul said to Tony: "I think I'm going to die."

The barber put shaving cream on Paul's face, got out his straight razor and honed it on his strop. He turned on the hot water in the sink and ran the dull edge of the razor under the hot water. He said to Paul: "If you're going to die, I'll help you out." He ran the dull side of the razor across Paul's throat. Paul felt the wetness from the shaving cream and thought Tony had slit his throat.

He went tearing out the front door of the barbershop like he was jet propelled. A car jammed on his brakes to miss him and was rear-ended. Paul ran straight into the side of a bus. Falling back, he felt his throat and realized it was a sick joke. He ran the two blocks home.

When the cops showed up, Paul was long gone.

Tony said he didn't know what happened: "Maybe some nut-case from the hospital down the street escaped." Tony owed Paul a few beers after that caper.

Paul died three years later. Doctors wanted to amputate one of his feet. He said "No way." He threw his needles and insulin in the garbage can. He held up two fingers and yelled "two points" for a perfect swish shot.

Claude

Claude was one tough dude, with a background similar to mine. We fought fires and knocked around together. Claude had two very tough brothers who ended up doing heavy federal time for robbery. Like me, he could have swung either way.

We both had strong, tough parents. Claude's mother told him if he screwed up like his brothers, she'd kill him. He got the message and never strayed from the straight and narrow. Crime was not his bag.

A tavern where we drank once in a while had a minor fire. The District Chief who responded to the call was a crusty man nearing retirement. As soon as he walked into the tavern he realized a small fire had been set in a garbage pail. He put the fire out and told the dispatcher not to send any vehicles. Then he told some punks to smarten up, and said they could have caused a major fire. They told him to go fuck himself.

The Chief left through the back door and walked to his car. Three punks followed him out and beat the living shit out of him. Real pukes. Real tough guys. They beat up an old man.

The next night Claude walked into the tavern and confronted the punks. They invited him outside. Their mistake! Claude went first and the three punks followed him. Claude kicked the first guy through the door in the nuts. He cold cocked the next one. The third one was meaner and tougher but Claude put him down and pounded the piss out of him. An ambulance was called and the third guy had to be taken to hospital for head trauma, a broken arm and six missing teeth. He damn near died.

The puke's father was a big shot lawyer and charges of assault, assault causing bodily harm and a few other odds and ends were laid against Claude. Conviction on any one of the charges meant the end of Claude's job.

That night, at 3 a.m., Claude went to the hospital. He walked quietly up to the fourth floor so no one would see him, and entered the puke's room. He was on intravenous, his arm was in a cast, and his eyes were almost closed shut from a broken nose and a broken jaw. When he saw Claude, he almost shit.

"Remember me, puke?"

The poor guy mumbled something that sounded like a yes.

Claude said: "I want to tell you something and I'm only going to tell you once, so listen up good. Your father's a rich, smart lawyer and mine is working poor. The Fire Department is family to me. I know it's no big deal to you but it is to me. Firefighting is my life. If you press these charges I'll lose my job.

I love my wife but she left me two years ago. If I had a choice between my wife and my job it would be a toss-up, but I think the job would win by a nose. It gives me pride and respectability. You know the pain you're feeling now? It'll be nothing compared to what I'll do to you if I lose my job! Do you understand?"

The charges were dropped.

Heroes With A Capital "H"

There are heroes and then there are heroes with a capital "H". Seven of my brother Ottawa firefighters fall into this heady category.

Steve Brabazon, Chris Whitney, Barry Blondin, Gord Thorpe, Brian Foley, John Hamilton and Mark Tedechini drove to New York on their own time and at their own expense to help with the aftermath of the destruction of the twin towers on 9/11.

The day the terrorists flew passenger jets into the skyscrapers, the Ottawa Fire Department mounted an immediate response. Buses were sequestered and preparations were begun to send as many Ottawa firefighters as could be spared.

Then word came from New York: STAND DOWN. The rescue coordinators were not prepared to handle the huge influx of volunteers from across North America.

Undeterred, the Ottawa seven decided to go it alone and show up uninvited and unannounced. They found they were most welcome.

Steve Brabazon and Chris Whitney have been in New York seven times for a week at a time and, as I write this, they are preparing for their eighth working visit. One Ottawa firefighter, a member of the Salvation Army, remained in New York a month.

All of the Ottawa volunteers, with the exception of Steve and Chris, decided to go to New York independent of each other.

Steve remembers his first time. After he was given security credentials he was taken down the ramp into the crater by a member of the New York Fire Department.

He said to Steve: "My brother is down here!"

Steve said he looked around but didn't see anyone else.

"I thought maybe I didn't hear him correctly so I said 'Pardon me? I don't see anyone'. He pointed to the ground and said: 'He's under there'. His brother was under hundreds of thousands of tons of debris with the 340 other New York firefighters who died. The pit – the crater – was huge. It was like standing at centre field on the football field at the Houston Astrodome and looking up at the top tiers of the stands. The New York firefighter said to me: 'Look at that!' I looked at what appeared to be a huge sandwich three feet high. I could clearly see the different layers. There were seven of them. They represented seven complete floors of the World Trade Centre. Down deep, if we looked at the walls of the crater, we could see the tunnel openings of the New York subway system and one complete subway car."

The seven Ottawa firefighters slept in their cars or vans or at the Salvation Army or New York fire stations. Once NYFD realized who they were, beds and billets were found for them.

Steve said the most unnerving thing was seeing NYFD fire-fighters and other rescue workers eyeballing the 16 acres of destruction and planting little orange flags here and there. Each flag represented a body or part of a body.

Their contribution was not restricted to on-site volunteer search and rescue. Back in Ottawa, Steve Brabazon and Chris Whitney cranked their sideline of silk screening T-shirts into high gear. They screened T-shirts with crossed U.S. and Canadian flags and bearing the legend – "FDNY – WE WILL NOT FORGET".

"OTTAWA FIREFIGHTER" was screened on the back.

The T-shirts sold for $20.00 each. Within three months, they had sold so many they were able to present a cheque for $30,000.00 to U.S. Ambassador Paul Celucci and New York firefighter Nick Giordano.

The entire story of the volunteer effort of the Ottawa Seven may never be told because they're too modest, too moved or too traumatized to speak of the horror of 9/11.

The story that hit me the hardest was told to me by Steve Brabazon. He met a young mother and wife whose firefighter husband had been lost in the first building collapse. Each day she was there waiting, watching and praying. One of my heroes found a piece of his fire coat and facemask – just enough so she could have something to bury. You have no idea how proud I am of these real men, real heroes! Most of them worked with me over the years and I am humbled by them, so very humbled. As I said, they were told not to go; they went anyway and God bless them for it.

Some of The Heroes I Worked With

There were men who served on ships in the North Atlantic when they were 17 years old, like Captain Lou Martin. He was and still is one of my super heroes; a leader of men, as I wrote earlier in the book. He was leading his men into battle at the Charles Ogilvie store fire on Rideau Street, when the building blew up and he was buried under a ton of rubble. His men gingerly dug him out. I got permission to leave my fire station in the south end and get his wife at St. Patrick's Church, to bring her to the hospital. He was a mess, but he lived. You look up the word man in the dictionary and his picture is there.

Another one of my heroes was Captain Al Owens. What a man, what a leader. He was a tail gunner over the English Channel at 17 years of age.

Captain Al Fraser was another exceptional man. He was in the Merchant Marine from 1935-40, the Canadian Navy from 1940-1945. Some of the stories he told were so sad they'd bring tears to your eyes, and others so funny you'd laugh uncontrollably.

Another role model was Fire Prevention Chief Robert (Bob) Trudel. At 17, he joined the Canadian Navy, and served his country from 1940-45. A man's man. His first child (a baby girl) had spinal curvature problems. Bob loved firefighting and transferred to the Fire Prevention Bureau, where he was able to work straight days, and help his wife Betty with Susan. This wonderful man and his wife also adopted a young girl and a boy to give them a better life. He and his family, I can proudly say, are still our friends today.

Lorne Banning left Canada to fight in Korea in 1951 with 19 other young men. Six came home. Here's a man who should have been Chief of the Ottawa Fire Department. He led men and fought in the hellholes of Korea and because he, like me, had trouble writing exams, he never attained the rank I think he should have had. Too damned much emphasis on the exam and not enough on what a real leader like him could do. In 2001, I was doing a craft show with my wife at Merivale mall when Lorne came up to me and proudly said: "Look at this, Jimmy, I got a thank you from the South Korean government."

He was so happy and so proud. I thought it was fifty years overdue. Each time I see him I still tell him he's my hero, and he truly is.

Others of my heroes were captured, tortured and beaten, and wouldn't talk about their experiences. These great men paid the price to save our country, and our remaining veterans are treated horribly today. That's a disgrace. If it were not for these heroes, we'd be speaking German, Japanese or Russian today.

Last but not least is my wife Sharon's Uncle George. What a great man. When his country called, he answered and put on a uniform.

When he left Ottawa to go overseas in the early 1940s, Sharon's Dad drove him to the train station. He was to get on a boat to England, sailing out of Montreal. Money was tight, but Eddie, Sharon's Dad, gave him a few dollars before he got on the train. The very first letter Eddie got from George went like this: "Hi Eddie, long boat ride to England and thanks for the money you gave me. I put it to good use. I got laid. It didn't last very long, but it was great. I figured if I caught a bullet, I didn't want to go to the next world without getting laid first. Love, your brother, George."

He is still alive today and Sharon and I love him very much. He's over 80 and one of my true heroes, and his wife Joy is just as nuts and wonderful as he is.

I apologize to the people I didn't mention. It would take hundreds of pages. Look for the next book.

Epilogue

Why did I write this book? Because, as an officer and a gentleman, I keep my word. If you picked up this book expecting great writing and million dollar words, put the book back on the rack and buy something else. I don't pretend that I'm anything other than what I am… a husband, father, friend and a firefighter. God didn't make me the sharpest knife in the drawer but he made me shine in other ways.

I love my wife of 39 years and my three wonderful children, and I love and respect my friends. The one thing that has given me pleasure, pride and pain was being a firefighter. God, how I loved my job and the true heroes I had the honour, privilege and pleasure to work with.

I was hired January 4, 1960, along with 33 other men. Firefighting back then, over forty years ago, was just about the same as it was 100 years ago – axes, pike poles and no air masks. Just get in, stay low and take a real shit kicking. Do a circle – it was really a square – get in the room, put your shoulder on the wall and feel your way around. If you found a closet you pulled things out of it. If you found a window you opened it or broke it to get some precious air in your lungs. If you found a bed you checked it and then tipped it over to see if a child or someone was under it. Children can hide in the smallest places. If you find someone, the taxpayers love you; if not, they think you're a pack of assholes for busting up a house or a commercial establishment.

My first winter on the job was the winter of 1960-1961. I was involved with 17 deaths. I was 20 years old, working with Second World War and Korean War veterans ... God's real super heroes ... not the comic book kind.

This book was written because I made a promise to Lieutenant Donny Gagnon. Who was Donny Gagnon and who cares? I care. He was a great firefighter and friend. Donny and I were stationed together in the early 1970's. We fought many fires together and we got along very well because we were basically loners. We gave the job 100% but we didn't curl, bowl, hunt or fish with a bunch of off duty guys. We were just old-fashioned family men. When I became a Captain, Donny became my Lieutenant. God, that made me happy. We had the best bunch of firefighters anywhere.

As I said to my friend and mentor, Pat MacAdam: "My men could walk on water." Our fire crew consisted of firefighters who had been in different kinds of trouble. I didn't care. I'd take them and treat them with respect and they never let me down. Donny was an athlete – a super hockey player. He was 5'11" and he was 234 lbs of tiger meat. He was invited to go to the Detroit Red Wings training camp, but declined because he loved his wife, daughter and the fire department, and couldn't bear to leave them. Donny fell ill and dropped from 234 lbs to 126 lbs in a little over a year. He thought he had cancer but it was diabetes.

Near the end of his life, I'd phone him every day to make him laugh or cry, depending on the stories I told him. In early 1996, he said: "Jimmy, I'm dying." I said: "Donny, you'll be around for years." His answer: "Jimmy, your body lets you know when you're going to die. I don't think I have 30 days left." He died 27 days later. Before he died, he said: "Jimmy, please write a book." I said: "Donny, I don't know how to write a book, I'm a firefighter." He said, "Jimmy, I have never in my 46 years met anyone like you. The gangsters, bikers and people from every walk of life who came to visit you over the years at the fire station. Some were just out of prison – I'm sure a few of them were armed. I remember when the head of a crime family came to visit and the Captain locked himself in his room! Jimmy, please write a book, promise me." I said again: "How?" He said "Write it in a firefighter's voice. Firefighters will understand. You're a lot smarter than you think you are." With tears in my eyes I said "Okay, I'll do the very best I can, and if it's God's will and the book is successful I'll buy a dialysis machine and donate it in your name and the Ottawa Fire Department's."

I bought a small tape recorder and started recording stories. A year later, while I was directing a fire in a three-door-row, all hell broke loose and a hydro vault exploded and three of us ended up in the hospital. On the way to the hospital the paramedic said to his assistant: "I think we're going to lose this guy." I looked around in a dazed state. They were talking about me. At the hospital I had intravenous in both hands and an oxygen mask on my face. A nurse came over to me and asked "Do you want to see your priest?" I said: "I'm a Protestant." She said: "Do you want to see your Minister?" I told her I was a member of AA. I told her I did believe in a Higher Power and asked her if it was that bad? She answered: "Yes."

I was not afraid to die. I'd lived such a great life. My family was picked up by the Chief's car to come and say goodbye to me. My blood pressure was 280 over 126. With blood pressure that high something should have blown – a stroke or a heart attack. But I lived.

The name for my post-trauma condition was Traumatically Induced Stress Reaction or Post Traumatic Stress.

My doctor, Eric Deernsted, sent me to see a psychologist, Dr. Doreen Gough. What a gift from God she turned out to be... She got me to write stories about my firefighting life. Then she took me off all medication. On medication, I was a walking zombie and when I did get to sleep it was like Edgar Allan Poe was in my head. I would have horrific nightmares and wake up wet from my knees to my neck.

Then a wonderful thing happened. My wife Sharon got in touch with Pat MacAdam, who had just written a sixteen-part newspaper series on bank-robber Patrick (Paddy) Mitchell of The Stopwatch Gang. Paddy and I have been friends since 1955. He went one way – I went the other. Pat MacAdam said: "I love your work, Jimmy. It's very visceral." I told him I was a product of the public school system and didn't know what visceral meant. He said: "Your work is so natural and it goes right into my soul. Your story about the little boy you found on the stairs and wrapped up in your fire coat – it put tears in my eyes."

I said: "Pat, I'm not a writer." He said "Write it in a firefighter's voice." Each week my psychologist, Dr. Doreen Gough, and I went through more stories. I would cry and get rid of the garbage inside me.

The clincher came for me when I visited my boyhood friend, "Paddy" Mitchell, in a federal U.S. Prison. "Paddy" was sentenced to 65 years in Leavenworth. He was North America's most publicized bank robber. "Paddy" took an 18-week Creative Writing course in prison, and he was writing his memoirs. He asked me to be his agent and manager. He also encouraged me to commit my life as a firefighter to print. "Paddy" impressed on me that if I could tell a story, then I could also write it. He reduced it to such simplistic terms that the scales fell away from my eyes. Three people, Donny Gagnon, Pat MacAdam and Paddy Mitchell all said the same thing: Write in a firefighter's voice.

If you want to plug in with Paddy Mitchell, he has a website: www.paddymitchell.com.

So here it is! I hope you enjoyed my life. I sure did.

Author's Note

Thanks for buying my book. For all intents and purposes, it is a catharsis of the soul and a cleansing of deep-rooted memories that I was able to bring to the surface and face.

One of my favourite performers is the great singer and master songwriter, Merle Haggard. I would have loved to travel on road trips with him and be his drummer but, at 65 years of age, this isn't going to happen. He wrote a song about me, unknowingly, called Footlights. The song starts off with these words… "I've lived the kind of life most men only dream of". That's my life. That's me. What a blessed life God let me live.

I remember the night – it was a Thursday – that I knew Sharon was the woman I was going to marry. I phoned her from the fire hall. I had Saturday night off and thought we could go nightclubbing or something. I said: "What are you doing Saturday night?" Her answer was: "I'm going dancing with my father." This was 1964. I was 23 years old and the answer stunned me. "Why?" I asked. She said "My Mother died of a double mastectomy a few years ago, and my brother was killed trying to land a plane on the Bonaventure aircraft carrier. His body was never found and I never allow my father to be alone." I knew that night that she was the woman for me. I love her so very much.

I have not always been easy to live with – I had many monkeys on my back, many warts and idiosyncrasies, but she stuck by me through thick and thin.

I not only liked my only real job. I loved it. I loved firefighting. The calibre of men I worked with is indescribable. Real men, not plastic people. Men who never had to worry about dying and going to hell, because they'd already been there. I had the honour, privilege and pleasure to work with them.

Most of them are dead and gone to meet the Lord. Some are still with us and I never miss our annual reunion dinner, so I can, at least once a year, be in the presence of greatness.

I hope each and every one who reads this book gets something out of it. Information about the wars we were involved in is not taught in our schools. Children are taught very little or nothing at all about the sacrifices men and women made, and how much we owe them. Remember: if you forget your past you are doomed to repeat it.

A published author friend of mine recently received an unsolicited compliment from his Publisher: "It's sad, isn't it, that we don't teach Canadian history in schools in a way that engenders respect for our heroes of the past. It's a pity textbook writers can't make these stories as exciting as you have."

Love and respect! Education is a wonderful thing when used properly.

In closing, thanks, thanks, thanks for allowing me to be your servant for thirty-nine years.

Retired Firefighting Captain
James (Jimmy) Allen

If you live long enough, life goes full circle. I had a friend in high school in the mid-1950s. He's a musician and songwriter. He went one way – to Nashville and other music hot spots in the U.S., and I joined the Fire Department.

Our paths crossed after an interview about me in the Ottawa Sun. He phoned the author of the story and asked if I was the Jimmy Allen he knew from high school. We linked up and have become friends again.

Out of respect for the 9/11 victims he wrote a song that tugs at your heartstrings. I am attaching the lyrics.

THAT SEPTEMBER 11

Words & Music by DAVID BRITTEN

That September 11, another day in infamy
Another challenge to our future, an attack on liberty
And as the buildings began to crumble
With all that humanity
The free world stood there and cried
With you and I

That September 11, we will not forget
It was a time for grieving for all those innocents
And for the firemen and policemen
Who try to protect us all
Yes, the free world stood there and cried
With you and I

And those moments of injustice
That were served to us that day
Would be a source of unity to guide us along the way
Let the power of love be stronger than the hate
that ruled that day
Let there be love, let there be love